# TOGETHER WE ARE NORMAL

# Together We Are Normal

KATHRYN AURELIA SCHELDT
& JOHN HEYWARD DOWDNEY

*Together We Are Normal*
Copyright © 2020 by Kathryn Aurelia Scheldt and John Heyward Dowdney

Cover art and interior drawings by Valerie Simosko
Book design by Danna Mathias

Hardcover ISBN: 978-1-7356905-9-9
Paperback ISBN: 978-1-7356905-7-5
Ebook ISBN: 978-1-7356905-8-2

# ACKNOWLEDGEMENTS

We are truly grateful for their direction and clarity:
Editors Jeanine Normand, Katrina Robinson.
Cover artist Valerie Simosko.
Graphic artist Danna Mathias.
Friends and confidants Frye, Marie, Jeff, Jane, Marti,
Stephanie, Tish, Susan, Kevin-Ruth, Kristina.
Jezebel and Sprocket.

# DEDICATION

*For Pamela Jane*
*KAS*

*For Sam and Matt*
*JHD*

# ABIDE

Faith of the flowers
Faith of all that lives and breathes
Faith of you and me

Hope springs internal
Inside where the seed is spawn
Look, and there I am

Love is a story
You tell yours, and I tell mine
Share in the glory

KAS 8/29/20

# Part One

KATHRYN AURELIA SCHELDT

# December 1971

DID THE BLOOD-SOAKED PARQUET CRY OUT?

She had opened the heavy door to the brownstone on West Eighty-Ninth Street. Her face was the last thing I saw before I passed out and the first thing I saw when I came to. The parquet was cold and hard. I looked up, meeting the alarm in her eyes, the warm blood between my legs flowing down my thighs onto the floor.

A petite dynamo, John's mother coaxed me into the bathroom.

There it was—everything John and I had been through, and had come to, and all that we were—expelled on the floor in my blood.

My body had failed me. My heart had ripped apart. My spirit was shattered.

This memory has been firmly implanted in my cells since I was twenty-one: my first and only pregnancy. My fear of not being good enough magnified in full contrast to the rapturous months, days, and nights John and I had shared. All of this… this and more…kept washing over me in a sea of remembrances and wild thoughts.

# Anticipation

THAT WAS FORTY-SEVEN YEARS AGO—AND THEN, a little over thirty years ago, a bolt out of the blue. John had sought me out by phone wanting to make amends, the ninth step in the AA program. At the time, I was living in Charlotte, North Carolina, married to husband number two. That's when John and I had started catching up.

Today, John is a father, a grandfather, a twice-divorced alcoholic with thirty-plus years of sobriety, and a cancer survivor living on social security.

My first true love—how would it feel to see him and for him to see me now?

*On July 2, 2010, at 4:15 p.m., JohnDowdney1@getmail. com wrote*:

Your birthday is one of the few I ever can remember. Happy birthday, almost a firecracker, and peace.

You enriched my life, and I am truly grateful. Love, John

*On July 2, 2010, at 6:02 p.m., KathrynScheldt1@getmail.com wrote*:

Hey, really great hearing from you, John. I think about you a lot and wish we could see each other and go down memory lane.

We're still struggling down here with the results of the oil disaster in the Gulf.

Hope all is well with you and your family. Love, Kathryn

*On July 3, 2016, at 7:37 a.m., JohnDowdney1@getmail. com wrote*:

Almost a firecracker…happy birthday, beautiful. Hope this day is filled with peace, joy, and love.

Looking forward to your visit and the tales of your journey through life. Oh, oh, and your music.

Have a great day. As you get closer, give me a call. Love, John

*On July 3, 2016, at 8:58 a.m., KathrynScheldt1@getmail.com wrote*:

Thank you, John. I will call from the road. Looks as if I'll drive your way August 5, arriving that evening. Will need directions, etc. Looking forward to it. Happy third, and safe and happy Fourth! —Kat

John had sent me emails that arrived annually to wish me a "you're almost a firecracker" birthday greeting on the third of July. It always touched me that he would remember me with such a kind gesture. This year, the email arrived with a picture of the marsh and a note announcing his new life settled in his mother's former summer home on the marshes of Mount Pleasant, South Carolina. He had invited me and my husband to visit him any time.

The timing of his invitation proved to be synchronistic. My annual solo road trip to Pennsylvania to visit Dad was coming up. On the way, my typical stop was in Atlanta to visit my sisters. For the return trip to lower Alabama, my stopover was in Camden, South Carolina, to see my lifelong friend, Pamela Jane. *This time, why not reconnect with John and old college friends living on the Carolina coast?* John's offer of hospitality had intrigued me. I was on my way. The door of my heart continued to open.

My departure from Dad's in Pennsylvania was early enough that the traffic rumbled smoothly around Baltimore, DC, and even Richmond, on through North Carolina. I ate candied ginger and stopped only for essential breaks of coffee and gas. Crossing into South Carolina, I waved goodbye to the countless, tacky, tourist-trap signs and breathed a sigh of relief.

Some twelve hours to drive in one day, with the unknown on the other end waiting for my arrival. Sweltering August heat matched my own. The burning desire of my heart, my will, and my mind propelled me down I-95 toward Mount Pleasant,

South Carolina. What would it be like to see John now? How would it feel?

The road opened, and it was the home stretch. But just when I thought I had it—the traffic came to a halt with no warning. My dashboard still registered 103 degrees, which had been the case all day. Traffic stalled for an hour on the Pee Dee River Bridge. Stewing in my own juices, sinking into acceptance of the obvious, fading from focused to a kind of mental mania and borderline exhaustion, I ate more ginger.

I called to update John again, this time reporting my delay. His voice was calm and comforting. Did he sound nonchalant? No second-guessing allowed. The end-of-the-road blues were getting to me. I cranked up the music and sang along till breaking free of the roadblock, back on track toward Mount Pleasant, crossing the tidal expanse of the Lowcountry.

I stopped to assess the road damage to my physical condition…grrr…worse than expected. And this would be his first impression of me? Not to mention the utter chaos of my car. Humbled by humidity hair and crumpled clothing, I briefly freshened up, brushed my hair, sprayed my face with rosewater, and put on some lip gloss. Turning on John's street, so ready to stop moving, I had already stopped thinking.

# *Arrival*

TOUCHDOWN. THERE IN THE SUNSET, JOHN WALKED toward my car. *It's okay now.*

He had weathered the years well, his ruggedly refined good looks housing the young Adonis I had once loved. We had a carefully measured "hello" hug. Popping open my trunk, I was embarrassed about the mess, making a lame apology. But John, in his well-bred fashion, simply toted in the necessities of one weary traveler.

He escorted me to the bedroom with a breathtaking view of the marsh. This was his room, but he had offered it to me for my visit. His touches of kindness were everywhere: dark chocolate by the bed and a single bay magnolia with a bamboo frond artistically placed in the bathroom. The door of his closet was off the hinge, and you could see directly into his summer wardrobe: khaki, button-down, Hawaiian print, denim. On his computer desk, visibly placed, was a page of Ingrid Bergman postage stamps. And there on the wall, looking back at me like an old friend, was the tiger. John's mother had framed his kindergarten painting and hung it in the Manhattan brownstone entry hall—a blast from the past. My nerves and excitement settled a bit.

Making a couple of brief calls to Dad and my husband to report my safe arrival, I heard John rustling up something in the kitchen and followed the food. He prepared a crisp salad with cold chicken on top. It was heavenly, jogging a memory of the many meals we had shared during our university days. In our supper club, we had engaged in regular gourmet dinners on a student budget, rotating from one hippie house to another.

I sat, lifted my fork, and looked at him across the table. *Be still, my beating heart.* The evening's enchanting crescendo unearthed Pandora's box of memories flowing in a never-ending dynamic. My body, from the top of my head to the tips of my toes, still knew this man—from the inside of my heart out. Falling in love with him all over again was so natural that I didn't even question my sanity.

After dinner, John showed me the plump white peaches that would be perfect by tomorrow. They filled the air with their perfume, nearly knocking me over, ardently redolent of our peach affair on a Macedonian beach. We remembered every detail. Our young love was forever etched in our DNA.

For dessert, we indulged fully in a fair-trade chocolate bar, which brought up even more memories. We laughed our heads off, recalling my "overdose" on Dutch dark chocolate when we were in Amsterdam back in 1971.

Too quickly, it was way past bedtime. We hugged each other goodnight and closed our individual bedroom doors, establishing our safety zones. The door closed, I felt alone—loved and alone at the same time. My heart raced like a wild animal in a cage. The closed-in feeling only made my heart beat louder. Was it the captivity of marriage?

My husband knew I was visiting a boyfriend from my university days. He had heard stories about John and the early escapades in Europe. My husband and I were best friends; and even though we were a couple, we weren't joined at the hip. We had a mature relationship.

I was determined to stay loving and clear with all parties. The soul's journey is personal. Was there enough love for all of us in this fragile equation? I was not showing up on John's doorstep like some unhappy married woman looking for an affair, which is what most people would assume. This meeting of old friends was overwhelming enough already.

I brushed my teeth, washed up, and made myself do the necessary ablutions to prepare for sleep. I slipped into the soft, smooth sheets, lay my head on the pillow, and closed my eyes. My heart was still racing. The road was still in my body. I had to get up repeatedly to pee. All that coffee wouldn't let me rest. Knowing John was in the room close by made me want to hold him and fall asleep in his arms as I had done so many nights in so many places, full of flying dreams and lovemaking of every possible manifestation. Meditation was impossible, but I drifted in and out of a trancelike review of years gone by until there was nothing between us except two closed doors.

When dawn broke with a honeyed light waking up the chartreuse sweetgrass, I was glad to pour myself into my legs and put my two feet on the floor. I tiptoed to the kitchen in search of the elixir of life, opening a cabinet to find a bag of Sumatran.

We had a full day and night ahead of us. A college friend was coming for lunch; but for now, the marsh called. I cut up the white peaches and poured cups of coffee. John joined me on the deck; and we stared out over the marsh, easing into a day in paradise.

Giant camellia bushes and subtropical vegetation provided a sanctuary of privacy, the perfect setting for being in a kimono coma. Approaching a sufficient level of caffeine intake, we gushed forth with questions and answers about the years in between: loves, losses, careers, joys, sorrows, successes, failures, therapies, recoveries, families, and friends, all this exploding like hot popcorn overflowing.

I updated John on my life in music from student to professor, from soloist to songstress, from academic writer to poet. How music was my common thread even though my theater marquis changed along the way, depending on what life either directed or dictated. The peaches were juicy and sweet. The coffee pot was nearly empty.

Out on the deck, surrounded by the swamp trees draped with Spanish moss, we searched our souls and let the music play. But time crept up on us, and our lunch guest was on the way.

Even taking a shower couldn't break the spell. The beauty of the single bloom John had placed by the sink held a love message not found in a cultivated bouquet from the grocery store. Standing there looking at my nakedness in the bathroom mirror, I was nineteen again.

It was great to see Bryan and John; they had never lost contact with each other through the years. We acted silly and took funny pictures. We telephoned a few mutual friends, now living far and wide, and talked old times.

After Bryan left, John announced his need for a nap. He said he wanted to be fresh for the evening ahead. Before censoring my thoughts, I said, "Could we take a nap together? I need to feel close to you."

He replied with conviction, "Oh, of course."

We walked into the bedroom overlooking the salt marsh and climbed on top of the covers. My head rested on John's shoulder. Our breathing came into sync, and in a few quiet moments, our hearts were beating with the same intervals. Light moved all around our bodies. It intersected with itself, connected and sparked, like being cradled by the Creator.

Looming out of the marsh, the sentinel oaks stood guard. Some of the most dangerous, exciting, and frightening moments of my life were the ones John and I had experienced when we had been young and in love. Yet during those days and nights, I was safe; and by some miracle, I was having that same experience. Being with each other was enough.

John continued to reveal his heart to me, how our love was the most intense he had ever known and how he had treasured it over the years as he journeyed to sobriety, raised his sons, cared for aging parents, struggled with career choices and his own health issues. Even though we never slept, the catnap was both restful and energizing. Time and space had not altered our essences. Our love for each other would not diminish but would augment our love for others.

# Departure

THE SUN SANK IN A RED AUGUST SKY. THE DAY was ending, and it became obvious that it was nearly suppertime. And my early morning departure was fast approaching.

John pulled out an iron skillet and cooked up a steak. With it, we enjoyed tastes of late summer: the sweet Pennsylvania corn and tomatoes I had brought. Our back-and-forth banter continued. We polished off the peaches.

Soon we were both yawning. It was a good idea to finish with a few bedtime stories. We settled into an embrace as close as the sounds of the night. With a soft, restrained kiss, we said goodnight again. Unlike the first evening, when we closed our doors this time, there was a tender peace which would lead me directly to dreamland. *Sleep will come.* The difference in waking and sleeping seemed like little more than a body position.

John was on task the next morning when, gratefully, the smell of coffee woke me. I staggered onto the deck negotiating a full cup in one hand and a hug with the other. Gradually approaching consciousness, we picked up where we'd left off the night before.

We knew we could go on and on like this, slurping our cups. Staring at the sweetgrass and palmettos, blurting out whatever popped into our minds, a fluid dance where we moved back and forth uninterrupted, no judgments or criticisms, not even any awkwardness about who was taking the lead. The morning extended, and we drained a second pot of coffee.

Reality 101 set in. It was already getting hot with a long drive ahead. I went to pull myself together, attempting to put on a face to show to the world beyond the marsh. In a little boutique where I had been birthday shopping, there it had been: a tomato-red, cotton peasant blouse very close in color and style to the famous one of my college days. I had to have it to surprise John. He loved it and took some pictures of me in the garden. Lack of sleep and lots of tears had my eyes looking like an albino rabbit's. But my reflection in John's eyes told me it didn't matter.

I studied his face with a vast palate of possible expressions, his brow tightening. He was concentrating on something. We were pulling apart. We both felt it. Looking one last time over the marsh, I said, "This is the perfect place to write. Why don't we write a book?"

He answered keenly, "Sure. I need to be doing something."

I exhaled. We would do this. We would tell our story if for no other purpose than to hold on to the thread. Maybe this was the right moment. I had not divulged it to anyone, not even my therapist. Had brushed it under the carpet—had told bits and pieces along the way, but not the entire dramatic arc.

John and I were ready. As we interlaced fingers, we saw our own selves times two. Holding each other close, laughing till we cried, crying till we laughed, the light of love igniting chills. Familiar and newly discovered.

I drove off, waving until he was out of sight. Before the end of the block, my gut was wrenching. Huge tears. Joyful tears. Healing tears. Knowing tears. We had made the commitment to write about all of it, which instilled in me a strength I couldn't yet comprehend.

Ten hours later, pushing the speed limit to join my husband for a swim by the bay, the driving was ending along with the day. "Hey, I'm glad you're still here," I said. He and the salty air welcomed me. I recounted my last two days in South Carolina and how John and I had decided to write a book; my husband nodded. I thought, *Kathryn, you are the luckiest woman alive, living and breathing and thinking only love.*

# Kathryn's Story

"IN FORGIVING OURSELVES, WE OPEN OUR HEARTS and minds to the whole world; and in doing so, our good works change from acts of contrition to expressions of love." John wrote that to me in an email in 2016.

It would take years for me to forgive myself for being young. It had been a willful time. A time dedicated solely to being in motion. I had to move on. From where I was and where I had been to where I wanted to go.

With Dad back from World War II and Mama fresh out of Southern Gothic, I had suffered a comfortable and sheltered Catholic upbringing. My parents were practically teenagers themselves, carrying their own unresolved issues. Being the oldest of five children forced me into a position of adult responsibility way too soon. As early as first grade, I was taking care of my younger sister who had epilepsy. It was as if her life and death were up to me. We slept in the same bed; and when she had a nighttime seizure, it was up to me to put a spoon in her mouth (that was what we did back then) and to alert my parents.

An expressive, jubilant child, I had to learn how to hide it, or get my bare bottom beaten with a belt by my father. Mama would pretend to spank me by hitting her own hand and telling me to scream.

It was either control or release. My father was climbing the corporate ladder, and my mother, the social one. Mama was advanced in her thinking, and Dad was too busy to think. The stress of supporting us five children while racially integrating the plant where he worked was only somewhat relieved by double martinis every night.

Sylphlike and precocious, I was sexually aware at an early age. My mother was sensitive to this, and she did what she could to train me to manage it. One day, she noticed that my breasts were beginning to develop. She took me aside and explained what my body would be doing next. When my period came, she went out and bought a six-pack of beer and a box of pink sanitary pads. Mama never drank, but we sat on my bed, guzzled beer, and giggled like little girls, celebrating my rite of passage.

After high school graduation, and on a music scholarship, I went off for two years to a finishing school in Virginia. Because my parents were divorcing at the time, I was vulnerable, not knowing where home was anymore. No one ever knew that one of my mother's friends stole my innocence then. It was rape. I couldn't talk. I stopped eating. I went into therapy and learned to breathe into a brown paper bag. I had to learn to eat again.

After my parents' divorce was final, the best Dad would do, if only to spite Mama, was to guarantee to finance four years' tuition at the state university for each of the five children. No more private schooling. The vastness of university life confused me: huge classrooms, long lines, and tons of people everywhere. I was lost.

By the time I had gotten to the University of South Carolina, I was a mess but ready for some expression of my sexuality, which up until that point had been hidden, disappointed, disgusted, and damaged. I knew my body was capable of pleasure, except that would require shucking off layers of mistrust, pretense, and frustration. Fashions and lifestyles were changing drastically. Jeans, bell bottoms, hip huggers, braless in midriff tops: the late sixties were swinging toward the seventies. It was exciting.

Then my high school boyfriend came back from Vietnam. Dressed like Audrey Hepburn in *Breakfast at Tiffany's*, I took a bus to the Charlotte coliseum to meet him. He drove up like Brando in *The Wild One*. He pulled out some pot and began smoking it. I took my first puff. We went inside for the concert. That was just the start. It ended up that the relationship my old boyfriend and I had hoped to restart wasn't working for either of us. Being exposed to happenings I had never dreamed of, I didn't think about my boyfriend anymore. I thought about Jimi Hendrix and the music. I was turned on.

Dorm life was a nightmare, prompting my sister Janet and me to find a cheap apartment practically on campus in a stately Southern home in a state of neglect. We called it the Senate

Street House. Four brightly painted mailboxes represented the four residences: students and professors living at the margin of society. Janet and I stood out on campus, literally, as six-foot-tall beauties.

Once, when we were crossing the Horseshoe, a group of guys approached, and one called, "Hey, are you girls with the Boston Celtics?"

Janet replied without blinking, "Yeah…one at a time."

I was her older sister, but she was my big sister.

Venturing out one evening, Janet and I went to John and Kristina's for a supper club gathering at their flat. Kristina, whose mother was Greek, was a boldly handsome young woman. John was the epitome of a class act: English lit major in tortoise shell and tweed. They were both from Manhattan families with upper-crust credentials, which fascinated me as a small-town Southern girl. Kristina's supper club meals were exotic, with unusual salads, spices, olive oil, marinades, and such. And John was most attentive to her needs in the kitchen and afterward when we'd all hang out.

The way he petted Kristina reminded me of how lovingly he petted their Siamese cat. I thought, *Kristina is fortunate to have John…someone kind and tender.* It was something I had not seen before in a man. It was a longing I would always feel when I saw him. He was tuned in to something. I was spellbound. He was different, and that resonated instantly with something I knew about myself.

Rumors circulated that John and Kristina had split up. Two days later, John appeared at the Senate Street door. I figured he needed to talk about the breakup. I hugged him, glad that he hugged me back. We sat, his hand in mine. The moment we touched, electricity filled the room. This was something I had imagined for a long time.

I was drawn to his good looks, his sensitive manner, his frenetic mind, and his infectious curiosity about life, other people, and our world. And now he was interested in me. It was as if we were transported into the bedroom. Our clothes fell to the floor.

John softly held my cheeks and tilted my head up until our eyes met. "God, you are beautiful."

We were lost in the flow. Through the sliver of space between my skin and his, our desire crackled like pinewood kindling. I wanted to take all of him inside me. I felt like the whole world was hungry for this moment and I was the world. My grip on him was lyrical. I remember how it felt having him there. I remember how it felt holding him in the deepest part of myself. How I loved it and how I loved him.

It was the first time I was ever met. I never wanted to stop. I understood why people say that when we give ourselves to each other, we find ourselves at the same time. That's what we had. I would never let him go no matter what. I would follow him anywhere. The world became the cosmos, and we *were* the cosmos.

# Live and Learn

WE HAD FOUND SANITY AND SAFETY IN OUR love. The pressure to conform was as confusing as our own urge to define ourselves. There was no turning back now. The fabric of our lives was dissolving. The Vietnam War, political unrest, and social revolution raged and ravaged the world around us. We wanted to get away from it all.

This newfound clarity and security gave me the courage to leave the madness behind. John and I wanted a world where we could nurture ourselves and expand our minds. We decided to abandon university and to travel to Europe with the idea of staying on a Greek island for several months. I was on board.

There was the money issue to be surmounted. I made a plea to Dad for one semester's tuition by convincing him I wanted to get a "real-life" education in Europe. He finally agreed to send me $600. John managed to raise $1,200 by selling baggies of pot in the parking lot of the local burger hangout. That tidy sum of $1,800 plus two round-trip tickets John had previously bought gave us all we needed to start our odyssey.

John's family had planned a vacation in the Catskills, and we would join them before our flight to Europe at the end of June. En route, we went by Camden first to say goodbye to Mama and the gang. John promised Mama that he would take good care of me.

Mama hugged me extra hard, saying she felt like a mother bird letting her baby fly from the nest. "You're ready to spread your wings, dahlin'." She hit the nail on the head.

"Thank you, Mama." I would not look back.

John and I drove away down the dirt road and past the rabbit tobacco and scrub oaks when we saw Mr. Truesdale pull up with a truck full of bushel baskets of peaches. Dad used to tell stories about his boyhood days picking peaches in Louisiana, where the white peaches were the most fragrant and delicious, and those were some good peaches for sure. But these were South Carolina's finest: Carolina gold peaches. John bought a basket at the family rate of five dollars. The golden beauties blushed and filled our car with the scent of Southern summer.

As we journeyed north, those peaches proved to be solid gold for us. Not only did they nourish us, but every time we hit a tollbooth, we were able to barter peaches for passage. This worked like a charm until we got to the Lincoln Tunnel. Welcome to New York, my first cultural shift.

When we left Columbia, we were traveling light; but we arrived at Twilight Park burdened with our bushel of sun-kissed, blushing peaches. John carried the huge basket inside the cottage and introduced me, his South Carolina girlfriend, to his family. It turned out that his mother had deep roots in the Lowcountry around Charleston. Surprised when she showed us to our room with a double bed, I thought, *How cool.* She was very modern for the times.

Meeting John's family, I wanted to do something nice. Since there were far more peaches than we could manage to eat, I offered to fix a specialty from supper club days: peach pies. I made four pies from scratch, lots of peeling and slicing. I arranged the peaches into the bottom crusts and placed pats of butter on top. Then I carefully peeled the top crusts from the wax paper, pinched the edges tight, and decorated them with a peace sign, which I cut into each pie. My sisters and I had always cut peace signs instead of stars into the tops of our pies. I brushed the dough with cream and sprinkled a light dusting of cinnamon sugar. Positioned in the oven, they were sure to be a hit for dessert that night.

The fragrance filled the cottage with longing. We were all looking forward to something yummy. I took the blistering hot pies out of the oven as we sat down for dinner. To cool them in time, I put them on a wooden ledge right outside the cottage in the evening air.

The climactic moment was nearing when I went to retrieve the pies. "Oh, no!" I screamed my head off. All four top crusts had been removed with surgical precision by masked bandits: raccoons. I was devastated.

John came running out and gave me a big bear hug. "It's okay, sweetness. We'll eat the pies anyway."

We brought the damaged delicacies inside, tears rolling down my cheeks, while he did his best to cheer me up. We spooned up peach pie, which was now more like peach cobbler. And after all, everyone ate the dessert appreciatively. John and I had made our love public, and his family accepted me.

The veil of night fell, and we fell into each other's arms with full tummies and fuller hearts. We held on tighter and tighter, closer and closer, deeper and deeper. I rested my head on his chest. He dug his fleshy fingertips gently into my scalp, raking through my hair and lulling me. Our love was contagious, and I dreamed of those happy raccoons licking their chops.

This hamlet was the perfect spot for our love to blossom, planted in the forests of Twilight Park. The setting was both elegant and rustic with winding paths through substantial maples and pines with giant ferns, and a swimming pool fed by cool mountain spring water. John's entire family was there: mother and father, along with his older brother, Stephen; Stephen's wife; and their son.

Stephen was a bit out of step with the rest of us. A Green Beret, he had served in Vietnam. One day when we were all hiking, huffing and puffing, Stephen showed us how to walk uphill per his Ranger training. "Keep your knees softly bent and sink into your pelvis. You move forward easier like that." Fascinated by the results, I still remember the way I learned to walk uphill that day.

# Dublin

JOHN AND I ARRIVED IN DUBLIN ON JUNE 27. Exhilarating and exhausting, my first overseas flight was also my first experience of jet lag. The Irish summer was fresh and green and in full swing. The air smelled of shamrocks, tea, tourists, and poetry; the city bustled. John had been here before, and I trusted him to be my devoted tour guide and loving sidekick. He had a passion for the land of Joyce and Yeats, and he looked at home in the atmosphere of his ancestors. His carved profile grew into the scenery.

It was late morning by the time we checked into our hotel, and the pull of gravity enticed me to assume a horizontal position. I went directly to the bed, pulled the covers back, and detected something I had never seen before in my life.

"Look…they have three sheets on this bed. That's weird, isn't it?"

John replied without hesitation, "Europeans are very civilized. That third sheet is so you can have a 'nooner'!"

I swear I kept falling deeper and deeper in love with this witty, wise, wonderful guy. *Let's crawl undercover and take advantage of those sheets*, I thought in my jetlagged stupor. It wouldn't take us a microsecond to come together—sex and jet lag merged into a nap heavy with surrender.

As we eased back into consciousness, John suggested that tea might be a good idea. When we threw on some jeans to go out, the maid was coming into our room. From the heart of my unworldliness, I whispered, "She knows what we've been doing."

"Yes, she sure does." John impishly placed his arm around my waist, and we bounded down the steps, heading off to take in whatever would catch our fancies.

And that didn't take long. We found the Guinness factory and drank the frothy brown brew, and we made love. We devoured ice cream cones with a square of Cadbury chocolate stuck down in the middle of the rich vanilla custard. And we made more love. We celebrated the morning with thick bacon, farm eggs, buttered toast, and tea with heavy cream floating on top. And we made love. We witnessed the Book of Kells at Trinity College, and it took our breaths away. And we made love again. We walked the southern coast, and the Dingle Peninsula, and immersed ourselves in the spiritual sanctuary of St Kevin's Kitchen, the stones, the sea, the green, the heather, and the sky. And we made love. Yes, we did. We made love again and again.

John and I were both travelers, both seekers. Sane or insane, it didn't matter. We were lovers of life. We wanted more. We wanted it all.

When I think back on Ireland, I think back on my innocence and blind faith. And I weep. The same old questions of "what if" and "why" threaten my sanity. But the answers are written in my heart. They are in my cells and in my soul. The sheer luxury of life's journey and the unexpected reward of being given a second chance invoke the very essence and mystery of love. Majestic, divinely bestowed, awe-inspiring. I will put these tears to good use. I will continue to suffer being the fool, and I will forgive myself once again for being young.

# *Amsterdam*

AMSTERDAM WAS WELL WORTH THE LONG TRAIN and ferry rides to get there. A mind-expanding city, it's a living work of art, creation in action. And we were head over heels for Amsterdam. First of all, I am a "lowlander." My Van Westervelt blood was stirred in the middle of what felt like family. Kindred spirits, smiles, and bicycles were everywhere. Busy, beautiful people emanated positive energy like vivid rainbows.

John and I pulled our bags down from the train and maneuvered over to a sign that said "Lodging" on a nearby building. In a split second, two good-looking, well-dressed men walked in our direction and singled us out. I am sure to this day—and with all honesty and humility—that John and I in love were simply the most gorgeous couple in the crowd that day or any day.

In perfect American English, one of the men addressed us to find out if we were looking for a place to stay.

"Yes." We nodded.

He asked us if we had any problem with the fact that they were a couple. We assured them there was no problem whatsoever. They escorted us from the station to see if the room suited our needs, and it was fabulous. Tastefully decorated with exquisite furnishings and fine Persian carpets covering the wooden floors, that room turned out to be the most elegant we were to have over the entire five months of travel.

Our Amsterdam hosts were tremendously accommodating, steering us in the right direction for scoring some black Afghan hashish to kick off the evening. Another night, they recommended an organ concert in the Nieuwe Kerk, a seventeenth-century converted church in Dam Square next to the Royal Palace, and wow. The sounds of Bach swelled from the grandiose, period organ, which took up the entire west wall, flooding the air with Baroque ecstasy.

The Dutch had it all going on. They had learned from the reformation. It was about the music. And now after centuries, the church was packed with people still searching for mystery. They were squeezing in and sitting anywhere they could fit.

John and I sat on the floor, and that's when the real fun commenced. I had never seen that many people inside a church. We fit in because most of the folks there spoke perfect English. Total strangers showed us a bond of friendship and humanity by passing us these enormous trumpet-shaped joints called spliffs, and we puffed away. The air was absolutely infused with the essence of Turkish tobacco and hashish. I was a bit concerned about what reaction I might have to the tobacco due to allergies.

But with such a friendly environment, peace and loving kindness were in the communal smoke where the music carried us away in this landmark place of worship. The groovy light show bounced the colors of the fugue from the gold and marble. We were as high as the angel's eyes looking down on us and smiling.

That euphoria carried us back to the intimacy of our room, where compliments of the generous hosts, a round, signature box of Dutch, dark-chocolate pastilles called to us from the bedside table. I plopped myself down and stretched out. John sat Indian style beside me, and we tore into it, ravenous in the afterglow of the hashish high. An intense, rich orgy of chocolate, the bittersweet discs melted on my tongue like a carnal sin. I literally could not stop. One led to another one, which led to one more, and then another.

John still smoked, and I still ate chocolate until the box was flat empty. We both cracked up like two kids in candy shop. Starting to swoon, I truly didn't know what end was up. *Earth calling Kathryn, earth calling Kathryn*, kept going through my head.

John must have seen me growing paler and paler, and with what I perceived to be a fiendish grin, he said, "Kathryn, have you ever seen a chocolate waterfall?" That was all it took. I jumped up from the bed, and in less than a second, I was on the bathroom floor, heaving. Lesson learned: my chocolate passion had limits.

I washed up and jumped straight back into bed and into John's arms. He pulled me close and kissed my eyelids. We turned out the lights. Tomorrow was already on the way.

Our home base was right in the middle of town, and we could easily explore Amsterdam's hot spots. The Red Light District didn't do much for me. I found it far more amusing when we stumbled upon the interracial marzipan brazenly displayed in a confectioner's window. Handcrafted with painstaking proficiency from the sweet almond paste were tiny little beds with colorful people making love in various Kama Sutra-like positions. The sweets were multiracial and integrated: blacks with whites with yellows with browns with reds. And there they were, taking their pleasure in the company of candied flowers, fruits, butterflies, cats, dogs, babies, shoes, houses.

Sex was as much an expression of life as anything else. That felt good. That felt natural. There was a harmony of elements. This little country had found unique ways of living in close quarters and tight spaces, maximizing potential while radiating joy of life.

Strolling along the pedestrian avenue by the Floating Flower Market, we caught another scenario that blew our minds again. A small truck overflowing with flowers stopped for delivery. It was peak morning-traffic time, and a line of vehicles quickly stacked up.

"Can you imagine?" John said. "When this happens in New York, people go stark-raving mad, sitting on their horns, cussing and screaming, flipping the bird." Here, instead, people on their way to work hopped out and briskly helped the man unload. It was cooperation in motion. Without complaints, they got back in; and the traffic flow resumed its rhythm, never missing a beat. Now, that was civilized behavior, we noted.

# Tripping

WE NEEDED A CAR TO MAKE THE JOURNEY FROM Amsterdam to Greece, and we found a little gem: a 1959 Beetle. It was the definition of "shabby chic." We bought it for one hundred US dollars. That's shy of six hundred dollars today—what a deal. We were proud of ourselves managing to wade through the bureaucratic process of purchasing it, registering it, insuring it, and getting the tag saying "Nederlands," which would identify us during our road trip.

We were on a big adventure into the unknown, or at least, I was. John had already been in Europe with Kristina, first to visit her father in Germany, and then they'd gone on to Greece. I was somewhat sensitive about Kristina, but it was nothing that John said or did. It was all in my head.

Ambitiously, we decided to drive straight from Holland through Germany, on the Romantische Strasse into Austria, where we would stop for the night. Thick forests were decorated with fairy-tale castles that nestled themselves into distant hillside towns. The twists and turns made driving a real challenge. Seasoned German drivers passed us at a lightning pace, and occasionally, they gestured at us, pointing to our tag, "Nederlanders!" We took it all in stride.

On an isolated stretch in the middle of the Black Forest, we accidently hit a rabbit that jumped out of the dense trees; there was no way to avoid it. We pulled off the road right away. The rabbit was still alive. I was sobbing uncontrollably, and John knew what he needed to do. He told me to stay calm, that he'd be right back. He fished around for his pocketknife and went off grimly to put the poor thing out of its misery.

Looking back, it's obvious why I had such a meltdown, aside from my ardent affection for wild animals. It was the insecurity I held inside about not being good enough, especially in comparison to Kristina. After all, they had been here as a couple, and I knew it. I had been afraid of losing John. How a memory of a little rabbit can trigger such feelings: the exams of life never end.

By the time we checked in at a respectable hostel in Austria, I wanted to take care of John with extra TLC and rest. It was going to be a short night with a long day ahead. We were both dog-tired; but at last, we settled, shaking off the road.

John hugged me, saying, "Oh, sweetness, I feel awful about the rabbit."

"Don't worry; there was nothing you could have done. I love you." As I said those words, I knew my heart had won over all my instincts of sheer survival. John would not hurt me. He could not.

# Yugoslavia 1971

JOHN AND I WOUND OUR WAY ALONG THE LEG-
endary coast of then-Yugoslavia. It was to be my first experience of
communism, and instantly, there was a subtle caution in the air,
especially in relation to foreigners. The historical and geographical
significance of the stunning Adriatic coast had warranted rivalry
for centuries. It was a bit remote from the Western world that was
familiar to me. On the plus side, it was less expensive than the
other countries we had visited, and our money went much further.

The dictator, Tito, had unified the Balkans after centuries.
He was attempting to promote tourism by authorizing local
folks to convert rooms in their homes to be made available for
tourists, and there were signs denoting these government-ap-
proved accommodations.

Before getting to Split, we stopped for the night in the countryside near Zagreb, where there was a large farmhouse with the

appropriate sign out front. A middle-aged man and his wife took us up the stairs to the second floor and showed us the room offered at a fair price. It was comfortable enough with a big window on one of the outer walls. We had a bite of supper, surprised to detect an Italian influence in the cooking. We were worn out but keyed up, anticipating the next day's drive to the coast.

After our lovemaking, I needed to pee, and I searched for the bathroom.

"It must be down the hall," John said.

I threw on my shift and went out into the hall, which was an interior balcony with a railing around it, overlooking the downstairs living room.

There was a scary quiet and darkness. It became more and more daunting as my need to relieve myself became more and more intense. I snuck along the balcony, searching for the door I needed, but everything was locked up tight. At the end of the balcony was the door at the top of the stairs that we had climbed earlier with our hosts. I thought, *It must be downstairs, or maybe even outside.* I turned the handle, and nothing moved. We were locked upstairs, and there was no bathroom to be found.

I scurried back to our room, clenching, and whispered frantically, "There is no bathroom out there, and we are locked in up here, and I've got to pee so bad, I'm about to die."

We looked around for a chamber pot or anything I could use, and then I saw the window with a wide ledge. I ran over to it, hiked up my shift, sat on the rough wood, carefully positioned my butt far enough to clear it, and all hell broke loose.

*Oh shit*, I thought.

When the steady stream hit the ground below, I was suspended between my thoughts and my instincts, and the instincts took over. The sound of my pissing amplified in the stillness of the night.

John and I tried to stifle our hysteria. Then we heard the storm of cursing and screaming in multiple languages coming from the rooms below. The pee must have cascaded right past their open window, making a terrible noise and maybe a splash or two, waking up the farmer and his wife. John and I lay in bed, shrieking uncontrollably.

Needless to say, we wanted to make a quick escape the next morning. We skipped breakfast, paid, and asked for our documents. I'll never forget that man screaming and gesturing at us while we ran to our car. We didn't understand one word he said, but by the way he was smacking one hand against the other, I think he wanted us to give him more money or something. We bobtailed it out of there as fast as we could, laughing the whole way.

"They should have given us our money back," declared John. "Damnation. They should have paid us to stay there."

I have told that tale numerous times over the years, and it always gets a belly laugh or two. After all, peeing out of a second-floor window in Yugoslavia with the love of your life is not something one does every day. Was it Aristotle who said we learn what we learn to do by doing? Anyway, the real-life education I had bargained for was turning out to be a blast.

One thing I learned is that those old Romans really did get around. They embodied "over the top." Visiting Split and walking on the polished marble streets through the ruins of Diocletian's Palace, still the very pulse of the town, was too wonderful for words.

Life thrived around and inside the palace, connecting everyday life to history. It was hard to fathom the power of a ruler who could command such a home to be built for him, more than just a beach or mountain house. He commanded Sphinxes to be brought from Egypt, and columns, arches, and towers to be carved from local marble and limestone. How many slaves did it take? Unfathomable.

Palms and lush vegetation lent a richness to the beauty of the pink-and-white rocky coast. To behold that translucent water, a blue I cannot describe, even today—being alive was enough. John and I walked the paths of timeless souls.

And then, there was Dubrovnik. Set like another gem in the Dalmatian coast, Dubrovnik greeted us with open arms. Lovers being loved back…beauty embracing beauty. Chamber music filled the air, adding a spark of magic to our strides. We danced on marble streets polished smooth as glass by centuries of footsteps in war and in peace. It was amazing that even the gutters on the sides of the streets were contoured smoothly from the marble. And while the terracotta rooftops heated up with the sun, the yachts of the rich and famous, snuggling in the harbor below the great fortress, waited for nightfall when the city sparkled like Christmas trees under the dome of a sapphire sky.

We meandered through narrow streets searching for supper and came face to face with fresh fish displayed in a restaurant window. There was one fish that looked like a red dragon. We went in and asked about it. Somehow, with sign language and eye contact, we understood it was a specialty of the region. It was served with a smile, and we savored in it the pride of the people.

Years later when war and discord devastated the country, it made me cry to think that anyone or anything could hurt something that beautiful. But in spite of the fragility of life, love is stronger than hate. And nature can be forgiving. Recently watching HBO's *Game of Thrones*, I thought I recognized the setting—it was filmed in Split and Dubrovnik, where John and I had tasted the same salt air as the emperor Diocletian.

# *Macedonia*

IN THE JOURNEY TOWARD OUR ISLAND IN GREECE, our souls and bodies entwined. All of time was our time. There was nothing separating us. The idea of a soul mate had not even entered my mind back then, and it took me a lifetime of experiences to understand the notion.

We were off for Macedonia well before dawn. We wanted to skirt around Albania, and that meant miles and miles of rugged roads to Thessaloniki. We found a hotel and checked in. Our windows opened to the sea, and we listened to the water and the breezes. We were exhausted, but not too tired to make love. (We were never too tired to make love in those days.) Then we crashed.

In the middle of the night, I heard John ask, "Kathryn, are you okay? What's going on? You're moaning and sobbing."

"I can't stop scratching," I whimpered. John turned on the light. I threw back the sheet and screamed, "They're eating me alive." The white walls and the white sheets were speckled with mosquitoes; they were absolutely everywhere. We panicked.

"Let's go down to the front desk and insist on another room."

The proprietor shook his head at John, came upstairs with a canister, and sprayed everything with what we were sure was DDT. He pointed to the windows. They were all open. He slammed them shut and walked out the door, still shaking his head.

Another lesson in life here: When windows do not have screens, do not leave them open if the lights are on. Evidently, we had done precisely that, and the penalty was painful. John guaranteed me that I would not die in Greece from a fatal mosquito bite like the English poet Rupert Brooke. We held each other tightly until the madness stopped. I'm sure we slipped into sort of a toxic coma.

Our hotel, perched where the rocky coast gave way to a sandy beach, was soon behind me the next morning as the sea beckoned, and I ran into the water in a flash. Like a creature of the deep being lured back to where I belonged, I swam and floated in the bluest, clearest, and calmest water ever. Swim team practices at the Camden Country Club pool and body surfing in the indomitable Atlantic or in the mercurial Gulf of Mexico could barely compare to playing porpoise in the Mediterranean.

Swimming always made me hungry. I ran back to where John was sunbathing on a hotel towel. He offered me one of the white peaches we had bought earlier at a fruit stand. I took my first bite, and the juice squirted all over me. It was out of this world: enormous, yielding, and ready. Before I could go back into the water to rinse off, John held me, kissed me, and licked the juice from my neck and décolleté not to miss one bit of my pleasure. It was a blessing for my skin. His smooth lips brushed my ear. "Let me taste you…yum…sweet and salty. Kathryn, I adore you."

I got goose bumps. I wanted him then and there. And it wouldn't be long before my desires were to be completely satisfied.

*Delphi*

"KNOW THYSELF" AND YOU ARE GOING TO KNOW the gods. It sounds simple. These words are carved into the stone entrance to the temple of Apollo. This is where Apollo overturned the rule of the goddess of creation, Gaia, when he stole the oracle priestess at Delphi. But her message still echoes where nature meets the heavens, in the dusty ruins on the Mt. Parnassus highland, ever evoking another time…a time when the voice of the oracle wafted its way and haunted the very trees: "Earth, womb, mother, snake, Sybil, dolphin, sunlight, music, poetry, power." Pilgrims who continue to travel to this mystical spot search for inspiration from the essence of the goddess through her laurel-scented vapors and visions.

On our way to Athens, John I stopped at Delphi to see what the oracle would have to say to us. What remains vivid even today, a technicolor memory, is our picnic walk through cypress-lined paths and otherworldly panorama until we arrived at the temple. How much did we know then? Were we god and goddess? How far, through time and space and dimension, would we each travel only to return to where we started? I was living, breathing, feeling, touching—absorbing everything. I knew without knowing that I knew.

"Know thyself…know thyself…" The voice of the oracle priestess whispered to Shakespeare: "This above all: to thine own self be true, and it must follow, as the night, Thou canst not then be false to any man." And the oracle priestess whispered again to T.S. Eliot: "We shall not cease from exploration, and the end of all our exploring will be to arrive where we started and know the place for the first time."

During those nights and days in Greece, John and I became fused; but when we split up after returning to the States, we were two souls on two paths. Years later when we were to reconnect, we would recognize that we were of the one soul on the one path. Was that what the oracle priestess was telling us? Through all the bigger-than-life moments and inevitable struggles, our hearts had remained faithful to each other. They had always been connected to the divine.

*Athens*

HOTEL CLEO WAS SET RIGHT IN THE CENTER OF Athens in the historical Plaka neighborhood. From the rooftop garden splashed with shocking-pink bougainvillea, we could see the Acropolis, particularly spectacular at night. The small hotel was owned and operated by Cleo, an attractive Egyptian woman with a gracious manner. This lively yet ancient city soon felt like home.

Athens. Athena. The city named for the goddess of wisdom, the creator of the olive tree, a symbol of peace and prosperity. Her shining temples heeded us like watchful eyes.

John and I enthusiastically explored everything we could. The classical ruins and labyrinthine streets were dotted with curious shops and restaurants. My first Greek fast food was the souvlaki, and I marveled at the taste of my first octopus: like lobster, only more delicate.

Sitting in sidewalk cafés, we munched on salty pistachios and gobbled honeyed pastries, sipping strong, thick Greek coffee, watching the fascinating promenade of people while several feral cats observed *us* intently. Our lives were charmed. We attracted goodness everywhere.

In spite of the fun we were having with Athena, we were eager to get to Patmos. The Athens air was thick with hot, crowded summer. On our breezy island getaway, we could just *be*.

We drove the trusty Beetle to the lot in the port of Pireaus, parked it, and said goodbye. It was a shame to leave it there, but what else could we do? We were sure we would never see that car again.

John and I bought a couple of deck-class tickets to Patmos, and we were on our way to paradise. But paradise came with a cost. The passengers traveling deck class were in an eating frenzy. It seemed counterintuitive, but they were adhering to the adage that it's best to travel on a full stomach. They had brought food of all kinds. We watched with disgust.

Soon into the voyage, the movement of the sea was already catching up with the passengers. Not wanting to go into detail about the sights and sounds, I will say that the puking all around us was sickening. It appeared to be par for the course. Every now and then, and with a cavalier attitude, the boat crew dutifully sprayed the decks with fire hoses. John and I had a hard time not freaking out. We swore that on the return, we would get a stateroom and spare no expense.

# *Patmos*

THE HARBOR AT PATMOS AT LAST APPEARED AF-
ter a ten-hour boat ordeal. Wrung out, we stayed in the port
of Skala for a couple of nights to recover. There, we happened
upon a restaurant owned and operated by the Pandelis family.
Mr. Pandelis was a pudgy, red-faced man with a large smile.
He had very few teeth (and the ones he had were gold), and he
acted as if he were the man about town. He advised us to go
to the local police station, assuring us that the chief of police
would know about a house to rent.

When we asked the police chief if he could show us something, he said, "Nay, nay," while shaking his head from side to
side. John told me that was "yes" in Greek, and I thought he
was teasing me. It sure sounded and looked like "no" to me. Yes
is no, and no is yes. It was all very confusing, and it was making
me sick. My urge to go to the bathroom stepped up a notch,

and I couldn't face another public squatter. I thought, *Please, God, I hope we find someplace really soon.*

The police chief took us to see a house on Grikos Bay. He leered at me, making me self-conscious. Taking advantage of the moment, he pulled me aside from the group by sneaking his hand under my armpit. He didn't stop there, moving to touch my breast as he steered me in toward the master bedroom. Revolted, I gave him a dirty look and edged away. He quickly let go of me. Then, feigning polite manners, he said something I perceived as "Madam, how do you like the accommodations?" If I had not been desperate to get settled in and have an actual bathroom, pitching a hissy fit would have been in order. But nervous and queasy, I thought, *Whatever it takes. Let's just go.*

The house turned out to be absolutely perfect. It was to be our love nest for three months, for a grand total of 150 US dollars. Fifty dollars a month was affordable for us. The house was barely a hundred meters from the beach. It included a three-acre farm, three goats, and three garden wells. It was fifty feet from the water cistern. There were three bedrooms, a marble kitchen, and a modern bathroom.

We made the deal with a handshake from the unctuous police chief and from the gracious Nephele Kalsa, the widow who owned the house. In our best Greek, we thanked them, "Efcharisto poli."

Then the proverbial shit hit the fan. Evidently, I had caught some intestinal flu. I almost passed out in the bathroom. Reaching the bed and shivering, I collapsed.

John was visibly concerned. "Oh, sweetness, I am so sorry. I'll be right back," and he tucked me in.

In a flash, he had returned with our landlady, Nephele. She was a vision of kindness, her shining face in stark contrast with her black mourning clothes. She patted me, saying something sweet. I drifted off, who knew for how long. When I came to, I was weak as could be. Nephele spoon-fed me a crème she had made from fresh goat milk, cinnamon, honey, and lime. It tasted like pure love. It was her scrumptious crème that nursed me back to health.

We spoke the common language of humanity. She told me she was named after the cloud nymph, Nephele. When I gained strength, I went to the kitchen and watched her make the crème while she patiently stirred the pot with a wooden spoon. She was insistent that I should eat nothing else for an entire week, and then I would be well again. She was right, and I would never forget her care.

There was the resident tuxedo cat, St. John, whose name was pronounced "Sinjin" by the locals. Named after the prophet himself, Sinjin the cat watched over me, too.

John took over full-time nurturing. He brought me breakfast in bed: farm eggs, honey, goat milk, and cheese that had been brought right to our door. Fresh baked, semolina sesame bread, still warm from the monastery ovens, was delivered by a boy riding his donkey. Our garden was full of tomatoes, cucumbers, eggplants, and peppers. Wild oregano and rosemary grew everywhere. And figs were ripe for the picking.

Clean sheets and towels were brought fresh and changed twice weekly. They smelled like the unforgettable rosemary used in the rinse water. Our senses were in high gear. Our needs were few. Our hearts were joined. We offered our love to the world. We had arrived where our dreams had led us.

# Flying Dreams

EVERY DAY WAS A DREAM—A DREAM OF FLYING.
This is where and when those dreams began. Maybe the re-
moteness of Patmos inspired visions as it had for St. John the
apostle. Or maybe it was the hypnotic scent of rosemary-in-
fused air. At night, my head next to John's, and drifting off, I
would enter that dreamscape. "Let me tell you where I go when
I fly in my dreams," I whispered. "Like Wendy in *Peter Pan*,
I fly so high...nearly touch the sky...yet I always come back
here. I'm swimming through the air, hovering low or flying
high, watching the world below me while I'm invisible."

I wanted to tell him what it was like to be free. Whenever
he drew me close and entered my body, he claimed me. Our
love dissolved conflict, leaving only room for light.

From the front of our house, we could see the island of
Samos and the coast of Turkey. I remembered Samos from

studying the Romantic poets in high school. The British Lord Byron, enamored with Greece, perhaps inspired by Samian wine, had given his very life fighting for Greek freedom, an epic hero on the page and off. Pure romance. It's the ultimate offering.

John and I did not have to fight any battles. We were living the bliss promised in the "Ode on a Grecian Urn."

Keats wrote:

*"Beauty is truth, truth beauty,"–That is all*
*Ye know on Earth, and all ye need to know.*

My nose woke me up one afternoon. "I smell the French fries, and it's making my mouth water." Everyone knew the minute they started to fry the potatoes.

"Okay, I'm hungry, too. Let's go get some fries," John replied as he slipped into his shorts. We scampered down, starving from our sex-capade. It was to be a delicious habit for the next three months. A short walk from our house, the little tavern on the beach tempted us to the evening meal.

We sat outdoors looking across the glinting, azure Aegean, and ordered a large plate of *pommes frites*. They were definitely not fried in shortening. The Greeks always used local olive oil and sea salt. It was such a satisfying meal, and often, it was all that we needed for supper. If we were still hungry, we could go home and slice up some tomatoes from our garden. Or we could order a plate of octopus, in which case Sinjin would join us, patiently awaiting his treat.

Every day the fishermen would set out to catch octopus in Grikos Bay. They would drop earthenware pots down onto the seabed in the deep water. The octopus would believe it had found a home and crawl inside. Then the fishermen would pull the pot up and remove the octopus, whose sad fate would soon be proclaimed. It took me a while to get accustomed to the very idea of—and the sound of—octopus being pounded to death on the big rocks right there on our beach.

Once, John and I were in the full throes of an afternoon delight when we heard a relentless pummeling coming from the beach.

"Beating it on the rocks tenderizes the meat," John groaned.

That pounding noise was horrible, but nothing could intrude on our merging with the moment.

Later, John reminded me that they have to pound the octopus to its death in order for us to enjoy this delicacy. I somehow managed to distance myself enough from the sacrifice to eat octopus to a fetish, almost daily. The outside turned a pale, rosy color in the boiling water. When the wiggly, pink tentacles were sliced, the sweet white meat was revealed, served drizzled with olive oil, a lemon squeeze, and an oregano sprig. It was luscious, to say the least.

It was during my virgin experience of Mediterranean life that I cultivated an enthusiastic relationship with love, sex, and food. To this day, I would prefer to splurge on a fine bottle of ultra-premium olive oil or a sun-ripened tomato than most anything. On Patmos, I might as well have been writing a doctoral thesis on this primal linkage of the senses by the total immersion method. And in my flying dreams, I was taking in the big picture. My perception of life continued to bloom.

The arid dirt path from Grikos to Skala was about three miles. It was the route we had to use to shop for essentials and to seek diversion. Oftentimes, John and I would eat lunch or dinner at the Pandelis Restaurant, where we immediately became regulars. The food was scrumptious. Grilled lamb, fish, octopus, garden salads, moussaka, pasticcio, stuffed tomatoes and peppers—all cooked to perfection and served with affection.

I wanted to learn how to cook Greek food. I asked in my beginner Greek, and Mr. Pandelis agreed in his tourist English to let me observe him and his cousin in the kitchen. He required me to come early in the mornings while they were getting ready for their busy lunch traffic.

Eagerly, I started the very next day, trekking down the dusty path to town. The morning light filtered through the wispy tamarisk trees, and oregano bushes sharpened the air. There were islanders on foot and riding donkeys, and we exchanged the morning greeting, "Kalimera."

Mr. Pandelis met my arrival with his big gold-studded smile, offering me a seat at one of the outdoor tables. He served me a small plate laden with olives, feta, tomatoes, and pepperoncini. A "meze," the island word for this appetizer, was always served with a little shot of ouzo on the side to toast the day.

After this interesting morning snack, I went into the restaurant kitchen, ablaze with kerosene-fueled stoves, every one loaded and pumping. But they didn't have their own ovens; they used the baker's. There were large trays of food flying in and out to the village bakery a block away.

The Pandelis kitchen sounded like a New York street at rush hour: burners hissing and bubbling over; knives hammering; pans, jars, and bowls clanging; a frenzied cacophony, everybody barking out orders and yelling as they dramatically fried eggplants in scalding hot olive oil; stirred big stockpots of béchamel and tomato sauces; stuffed bright-red tomatoes and shiny green peppers with rice, lamb, and mint; and chopped and diced onion, garlic, parsley, and oregano.

It was an artist's studio, a kind of alchemy the way they shaped order from the chaotic environment. This symphony of spices with bounties from earth and sea was offered like blessings every meal.

## Sinjin

OUR ISLAND, PATMOS, REMAINS A FAVORITE PIL-
grimage site. Here, the monastery of St. John sits on the top of
a nearby hill, Chora. One can make the climb by foot or with
donkeys, which were always obtainable nearby. John and I had
often walked the trail. On the way to the summit, we would
pass the cave of the apocalypse, reputed to be the very place
where St. John had his vision of the New Jerusalem.

The stone citadel crowns the whitewashed city like a wedding cake, and the eleventh-century monastery even today ex-
presses wisdom and faith. Relics, bones, icons, and parchments
are safely housed and protected by the monks. There must be
secrets and puzzles, too, but much of the knowledge that the
long-bearded monks treasure benefits the community.

Besides a solar, salt-water conversion plant, the monastery
includes three sixteenth-century windmills (which were to be

restored to full-working order in 2009). The good works of the monastery and the island inhabitants continue to attract the devotion of an international community, everyone giving what gifts they can. Their beloved prophet revealed to them that when one works every day to make the world a better place, one works for a universal spiritual goal: "And, behold, I come quickly; and my reward is with me, to give every man according as his work shall be" (Revelation 22:12, KJV).

John and I didn't know at the time that we were doing our own work, novices on spiritual journeys, dancing through it all, ignorant of how hard it would get.

But living on Patmos was transcendence. I smile to think that we were in the prime of our hormonal harmonics. Oh, the advantages of youth and health and freedom that we could take for granted. Our expressions of love were completely natural.

The relaxed pace of quotidian life on Grikos Bay was often punctuated very colorfully. One morning, we heard a blood-curdling screech. We scrambled out the door to see what was going on. "Oh, shit, I can't believe this," John exclaimed. "Poor bastard, how in the world? How in bloody hell are we going get him out of there?"

Sinjin the cat had fallen down into the well right at our doorstep. The deep-water well filled up a basement-like space under the house. The portion outside was rectangular with a metal ladder going down about ten feet into the well. Our little buddy was clambering and falling, clawing up and sliding back on the slick metal ladder, caterwauling frantically and causing general pandemonium.

While John reassured Sinjin, I yelled, "Back in a sec," and ran as fast as I could over to the tavern.

The tavern family must have thought I was crazy, bursting in breathless. I tried to explain, mustering every would-be communication technique to convey the urgency: my few words of Greek, some theatrical gestures, and even some cat language, which made them laugh. They shook their heads side to side, which no longer confused me, and enlisted their teenage son to help. He and I ran all the way back to the house.

"It's okay, boy. I'm coming to get you," we heard John say as he gingerly climbed down the rounded rungs into the pitch-black well, his toes clutching onto his flip-flops.

Too frightened to watch, I didn't know what to do. "Oh, John, please be careful. Don't fall in the well, too."

John pulled a plastic lighter from his pocket and clicked it. With that tiny flicker of light, we could see the poor cat. John continued to cajole, "Come on, boy, it's okay." At last, John cradled Sinjin securely in his arms and, one slippery step at a time, climbed the ladder until he could hoist Sinjin, passing him up to the young man, who gave the wriggling, wet cat to me.

Sinjin looked a fright, like a drowned rat—oops, I mean cat. His vanity was wounded. We attempted to dry his fur, but that didn't last long. He shook himself free and pushed away. When he turned and meowed at us, I'm sure he was thinking, *I'll lick* myself *dry, thank you very much.*

Back in the present time, *Forbes* magazine recently featured an article reporting Patmos to be one of the most unspoiled places to live. An island Zeus allowed to emerge from the sea; to this day, it's without an airport. Travelers must arrive by boat. Now, would it even be possible to return to Patmos? This has been in the back of my mind over the years.

# Leaving Patmos

DURING THOSE MONTHS ON PATMOS, JOHN AND I discovered a lot about each other and our childhoods. We had even invented the same game. I caught lightning bugs and put their brightly lit bodies in my belly button, decorating myself and parading through the summer night air. They illuminated my movements, and in my mind, I became a famous exotic dancer. John and his cousin Lisa had played a similar game.

John and I saw the absurd humor and joy of it all. We cried when we grappled with each other's pain. We both had shouldered physical, emotional, and sexual abuses in our pasts. Although our hypervigilant passion for life made us feel different from others, a compelling force of empathy drew our very sinews together. Our vibrational frequencies had become a unified field.

All the same, we had the DNA of melancholy. We were kin to the poet and the poem, the singer and the song, the dreamer and the dream. We had been hiding behind shadows, breaking free only when the note or the word or the picture or the tree or the sky or the bird cried out to us, saying, "I am alive." In Greece, we danced on sacred ground.

What we learned on Patmos was more valuable than what was taught in universities, and I had made good on my gamble about interrupting my studies. Yes, we knew what it felt like to be hurt, to have our innocence stripped from us, to feel shame and self-loathing. To feel isolated. But together, we were no longer alone, and we had found a magical remedy: trust. We weren't afraid anymore. We loved everything because we loved each other completely.

October was the last month we would spend on Grikos Bay. The little pebbles on the beach had grown chilly. I wanted to soak up those last bits of sunshine. I knew I had never been more beautiful. My sun-streaked hair hung to my waist. My body had more curves. I was a woman. And the season had begun to change.

"I want to hold you all night long," John said, and my eyes welled up. We knew we would be leaving Patmos the next morning.

I snuggled into his arms, saying, "Hold me so tight that tomorrow will never find us." Softly, I slid the soles of my feet down the front of his strong, racehorse legs, lengthening until I found the tops of his toes. We stretched and slithered in a synchronized, endless wave.

"Someday, we'll come back. Don't worry, Kathryn. Please... please...no tears. Kiss me. Hold me," John murmured.

I rolled over, reached for him, and our sighs descanted and escalated the tidal rhythms of that last night on Grikos Bay.

# Back to Athens

THE STATEROOM WAS WELL WORTH THE EXTRA penny. We could nurse our blues in near luxury all the way to the mainland. Wearing the glow of our beautiful island, we watched Patmos disappear behind the horizon.

When we arrived in Pireaus, we went straight to the old parking lot.

"Can you believe it? It's still here," John boasted. "Let's see if it will start." All we heard was the empty sound of a dead battery. "Fuck. Oh, wait a minute. Kathryn, you get inside, and I'll push."

I climbed in, released the emergency brake, and put it in first. John ran behind, pushing us toward the exit from the lot. I popped the clutch, and voila! Our little Beetle was up and running. I scooted over to the passenger's seat, John hopped in, and we drove off, our fate to the winds. The auspicious resurrection of the Bug was just what we needed to make it easier to let go of Patmos.

# Nutshell of the Current Me

BACK TO THE NOW: ANOTHER DECEMBER 31 CAME and went. The last fire of 2016 fading to embers, I threw in a stick of cinnamon and watched it burn away, quietly releasing the past year. The air filled with sweet spice. I embraced the year ahead: another chance to get it right. More time to love.

After all, 2016 was the year John came into my life as more than a memory—a vibrant force charging my neurons, setting the stage of daily life in a vastly altered arena for this brand-new year of 2017. Much has happened through the years since long ago when we were kids in love. Looking back, if I could have stopped the clock on Patmos, I would have. I wish I could have spared us the long years of struggle.

After we returned to university, I watched John and my friends getting wrapped up in the drug and alcohol culture. It wasn't for me. And it wasn't pretty. I needed pretty. I *need* pretty. I worked hard to master pretty. I chose the path of a classical musician. Music always gave me a place to put my emotions, and it would continue to direct me and to connect me with a vast universe of creativity.

The first boyfriend I slept with after John and I split was a good-looking guitarist. He was attracted to me, maybe a bit obsessed with me, and he wanted to own me. I was afraid of getting pregnant again out of wedlock, and I wound up marrying him. The marriage barely lasted a year.

Then it was off to Europe again once I finished my undergrad degree. Living *la dolce vita*, I did a bit of everything. After returning from Europe, I tried marriage again. It took me almost eleven years to come to understand that this husband didn't want children and that he drank way too much.

Nevertheless, during these times, I persisted, earned a master's degree, and established my music career. After my second divorce, that ex sent me a letter of amends. Around the same time, John contacted me when, coincidentally, he was working the same AA step.

Control...release...control...release. Some strange pattern had become habitual. I wanted to know why, and I wanted to know what to do to stop it. I wanted to make a happier and more authentic life for myself. It was as if the world closed in on me, forcing me to question my choices.

The nightmares wouldn't stop. I was breathing into the paper bag, but that wasn't enough anymore. In Jungian analysis, I dug in to the abuse issues with my therapist, especially the nightmares. I explored hypnosis, journaling, talk therapy, movement reeducation, yoga, meditation, prayer, nutrition, and exercise. And I took advantage of conventional medicine, too.

The hurt wouldn't go away, but I was gaining skills to manage it whenever it reared its ugly head. It intruded less and less frequently. I forgave myself. I forgave the abusers. I forgave the world.

By constructing new patterns and regaining my balance, I could give to others without giving away my power. After years of trying to convince myself that my work was what mattered, at last, I was able to be grateful for being born a beautiful woman with a brain. I was not just a pretty face—not that there was anything wrong with that. My voice came back. I could sing again. My heart wasn't shut down anymore. I was coming home to me.

Then my third husband came on the scene. He was independent and still a bachelor. He would do anything for me, and he demonstrated it. The marriage lasted twenty good years. During that time, my creative life was fertile. My partner was my friend. We went through cancer, deaths of parents, recession, depression, and other trials, while remaining our true selves. And what we still want is what is best for each other. We are grown-up adults.

When I saw John in August, it was evident that at last, he was a grown-up adult, too. What I mean by being a grown-up is to take responsibility and to continue doing the work. The exams of life never stop. It's about loving life every living moment. Love *is* all you need. And we each do our part.

Making a pilgrimage begs company, and eyewitnesses must tell it to those who have not or cannot go in person. John and I had made our pilgrimage together, and then, we returned home to forge our own lives. Last August, we decided we would tell our story. We would preserve it. We would tell it through our own eyes. Through our own lives.

# Back to Athens Again

NOW, I FEEL LIKE I'M IN A DICKENS TALE AS I travel through time with ease. Memories pour forth. It's apparent that the gods and goddesses had continued to favor us. And I go back to Greece in 1971 and to the youthful elation John and I had felt when our Beetle obliged us and we rolled out of the parking lot in Piraeus, windows down, hearts and minds open.

A mile or two into the drive, John looked at me, saying, "I have a great idea. Before we go back to Athens, let's hit the Peloponnesus peninsula. We might as well spend the rest of our drachmae, and it's supposed to be incredible."

"Sure. After all, we have time to spare," I replied.

"Okay, let's do it. Let's head for Sparta. That's where those hellacious warriors were trained. Not to mention, the home to history's most beautiful woman—except for you, of course,"

John extolled. Reciting his modified Marlowe, "Is this the face that launched a thousand ships and burned the topless towers of Ilium?"

I looked back at him and his wicked little smile. "Yes, it is."

The astonishing resuscitation of the car was to propel our pilgrimage even further. We were off again, traversing the breathtaking Isthmus of Corinth, winding toward the Peloponnese on our way to Sparta.

First stop, the ancient city of Corinth. John and I walked and talked for hours around the sprawling ruins that rule over the limpid gulf. When we came upon the Bema where St. Paul spoke to the Corinthians about his revelations, we saw a large stone inscribed with text, first in Greek and then in English. John leaped up onto the Bema, waxing poetic, reading aloud from the carved stone:

"For this slight momentary affliction is preparing for you an eternal weight of glory beyond all comparison" (2 Corinthians 4:17 KJV).

John must have been feeling the spirit, and for sure he was most entertaining, not only for me, but for the passersby as well. And in his own words, he continued, "My friends, understand that love is an action verb. Without the verb, the noun doesn't exist. Everybody wants the noun, but few act to manifest."

There he stood, all twenty-one years of self. He looked cute in his fisherman sandals—all muscular, suntanned, and sun-bleached.

"You're crazy," I said, "but actually, I think you have true potential." I took his hand, the same hand that had been madly gesturing when he had expounded on Corinthians.

What an uncanny feeling it is, going back in my mind, jogging my memory once again by visualizing these scenes. Cells spark and waves of sensation fire from head to toe. For all of these forty-seven years, in one way or the other, I have had a continuing love for John across the miles and the pathways of light.

# Uncanny Unearthly Acoustics

IN MY SMALL-TOWN, SOUTHERN-GIRL LIFE, I couldn't have imagined the wonders of Mycenae. Even though I had studied the Bronze Age, there's nothing like the real thing. Standing magnificent are the Rampant Lions at the gate of the city. From that first moment I saw them and ever afterward, they have stood like pillars of support for my soul. I hadn't known that lions roamed in Ancient Greece and throughout Europe. In Mycenae, they were immortalized: that noble pair, boldly enduring the colossal stones, guarding the entrance to the famed city for over three thousand years.

And what treasures were in their coffers to protect. I had never dreamed of such intricately crafted gold. John, like a good New Yorker, had shown me the Cartier and Tiffany windows, but they couldn't hold a candle to the Mycenaean gold.

It was a spooky feeling to walk into the dim light of the museum and to see the shining visages of the royal golden death masks. What civilization could revere their dead by burying them in such rich attire?

Peering into the display cases of jewelry, I was bowled over to find a large, gold brooch in the shape of an octopus. What meaning did that have? I, myself, had developed a near reverence for the octopus but had never dreamed of honoring one in ornate gold. Here was this sea monster of the depths brought into the light of awareness by some artistic genius. Once again, the Universe as I had known it continued to spiral and swirl.

After John and I left the museum, we explored the remote honeycomb tombs. We wanted to experience being inside the tombs of King Agamemnon and his wife, Queen Clytemnestra. History explains how the king sacrificed their daughter, Iphigenia. The queen avenged their daughter's death by killing the king. Queen Clytemnestra was proven innocent of her crime by convincing her accusers that her murderous act was necessary in order to end a cycle of violence. She was a true daughter of Sparta.

John and I walked toward the center of one of the two massive beehives of domed stone, our footsteps becoming increasingly louder until we reached the very heart. We could almost hear it beating, an unearthly acoustic phenomenon, some deep understanding of harmonics or, perhaps, the music of the spheres, creating an echo chamber of sorts. I couldn't resist singing. My voice extended throughout the space and stretched across time itself. John, awe-struck, gave me a round of applause that sounded like hundreds of clapping hands. Even today, I can will my feet on that sacred stone floor beneath me and experience those remarkable vibrations coming through my body. When we left that tomb, our footsteps followed us with the dying drumbeat of a thousand ghosts.

We carried on to Ancient Sparta, and it was quite Spartan: a sunken amphitheater in ruin surrounded by olive trees and grazing sheep. This civilization was dedicated to building strong warriors and strong women. It looked very different from the Mycenaean one, which produced something more lasting, like art. Once, I had bought a scarf from a boutique in South Carolina. On the tag was handwritten, "Ars longa. Vita brevis. Art is long. Life is short." It turns out that the quote is Hippocrates. Greek. Surprise, surprise.

## Olympia

JOHN AND I CONTINUED TO BE FLABBERGASTED that our car kept cranking up for us. After we left Sparta, we were running low on cash, and we would need to be heading back to Athens—and then home—but it didn't seem fair to go sporting about the enchanting Greek countryside without going on to Olympia for a fond farewell.

En route, we spotted a few cars pulling away from some roadside attraction where lamb was roasting on a spit. We could smell the barbeque. A man was seated at a wooden table covered with newspapers, a stack of them at his feet. Resting on the tabletop was another leg of lamb that he was carefully chopping into bite-size morsels with a little hatchet. After he had chopped the lamb into chunks, he scooped it into cones fashioned from the newspaper, serving it like the tasty fish and chips that John and I had eaten in Dublin.

Before the roadside chef gave me my cone, he walked behind the table and bent to pick some fresh oregano, which he crumbled over the top of my lamb like a priest sprinkling holy water. Sparkling eyes and furrowed face, he raised his eyebrows in a big smile when I thanked him in Greek, "Efcharisto poli."

It was the honest flavor of that juicy lamb, sustained on wild oregano, heartily prepared yet humbly served in newspaper cones, that made us swear that it was the most delicious lamb we had ever eaten and that every bite of lamb since then has been a disappointment. It's intriguing how food and memory do go hand in hand.

John wasn't as keen on seeing Olympia as I was. He was likely humoring the jock in me. My childhood mornings through high school were spent at swim practice. Mama would load the five of us into the wood-paneled station wagon to drop us off at the country club. I intensely disliked the competitions but relished the discipline of daily athletic training. Swimming came naturally for me. It was a place where the world disappeared, putting me in the zone.

My six-foot-tall frame gave me certain advantages for swimming, and it allowed me also to switch with ease from ballet to modern dance. I flatly refused basketball and other ball games. But once in the water, I became one with an alternate reality, luxuriating in the pure pleasure of moving through space like some mythic being not quite human, like some being that knew exactly what to do. I had won enough trophies, but that was irrelevant to me.

Swim meets were holy hell. It always made me sick to my stomach before the heats, standing on the swimmer's block, toes curled, poised like a cocked gun, ready, vigilant…waiting…waiting…waiting…diving in and then swimming like mad mostly to get it over with.

All the while, Mama was screaming at the top of her lungs, "Pull, Kathryn, pull, pull!"

I wanted to please my mother, but at times, she could go overboard.

When my figure started to blossom, she wanted to pad my tank suit. She didn't want me to feel embarrassed by having small breasts with curious nipples.

"No, Mama, padding would slow down my speed," I told her adamantly.

My short career as a competitive swimmer came to an end my senior year of high school. In fact, my life nearly ended as well. The events leading up to it coincided with my also brief reign as a beauty queen. That last year of high school was the first year of the Miss Camden pageant. In such a small town, there was a limited supply of eligible young women. Local dignitaries begged Mama to put me in the competition. After all, there was scholarship money involved. I balked and stammered, but they eventually talked me into being a contestant.

Mama took my friend Pamela Jane with me, and we got my evening gown and bathing suit. "Let's go shopping for some pumps, too," Mama said. "We'll probably need to get them dyed to match that lemon yellow of your bathing suit."

At that point, I nearly lost it. "Mama, I am not wearing heels with my bathing suit. That's insane. Swimmers don't wear high heels with their suits."

"But, Kathryn, dahlin', they will disqualify you for that," she pleaded.

In those days, all those beauty contests required a swimsuit competition, which to me was like a meat market. Waltzing around in a bathing suit on stage in front of an audience was ridiculous, and it embarrassed me.

I muttered back, "Okay, Mama." But my obedience wasn't absolute.

Pamela Jane was backstage styling my hair while I adjusted my one-piece swimsuit. There on the floor against the wall, looking up at me, were those perfect pumps, the yellow satin calling to complete my look, but I could not bring myself to put them on.

"Come on, Kathryn, it's only a few minutes," Pamela Jane sweet-talked me.

"Dang, Pamela Jane, no way. I know I promised Mama, but it doesn't make sense to me. I can't do it. I won't do it," I said, sailing out on parade, the swimmer I was born to be and barefoot as my one-eighth Native American blood decreed. There might have been quite a few gasps coming from the audience.

And there were consequences. I won the talent portion by singing and accompanying myself on guitar, "Easy to Be Hard," from the then-new 1967 musical *Hair*. For the overall Miss Camden competition, I only won first runner up. Mama was right. But so was I.

Mama was my biggest fan. She always championed my musical and athletic talents. Although shortly after the pageant, my competitive athletic pursuits were dealt a fatal blow at the Junior Olympics, and not for the reasons one would think. They were held in Lancaster, South Carolina, the home of Springmaid Sheets, where the athletic park advertised with brightly colored flags. Instead of Old Glory, they were boldly emblazoned with the legendary Springmaid Sheet Girl, waving from the numerous flagpoles.

A nerve-wracking day, the pressure was on. I held the fastest time in breaststroke, and I would compete with my relay team as well. After winning the qualifying heats, and in order to rest up for the finals later that evening, I was lying on the hillside relaxing.

Mama came over to tell me about her experience in the stands earlier. "Kathryn, I swear. Some people. There was a lady from Sumter whose daughter was in the heat with you. This lady was obnoxious. She went on and on about her daughter." Mama mimicked her, re-enacting the scenario in the voice of the other mother, "'I know my daughter will be the winner. I gave her filet mignon for breakfast.'" Mama looked at me. "Kathryn, can you guess what I told her? I told her, do you see that beautiful blonde on the block? Well, that's *my* daughter, and *she* is going to win because she had filet mignon for breakfast, too. But I served it to her raw."

We both cracked up. Mama did have a way of speaking her mind. She gave me a hug of encouragement, saying, "Now, rest. And here's a chocolate bar. Remember to eat it right before you swim tonight. Love you, dahlin'. This is your race."

After that pep talk, I drifted off for a power nap on the grassy knoll.

The next thing I remember is seeing blinding stars light up against the black recesses of my mind. As my consciousness was slipping away, I thought, *The bomb must have dropped, and it's the end of the world.*

When I woke up in the emergency room, Mama was there, petting me and mothering me. "Thank you, God, for protecting my beautiful girl. Oh, Kathryn, you're going to be okay."

"Mama, what happened?"

"Don't worry, dahlin'; it's over now, and you're going to be just fine. That's all that matters."

"But what about the finals?" I asked through tears.

"Well, sweetheart, some boys were shimmying up the flagpole to steal one of the flags. That made the pole fall. And when they jumped off, the flagpole landed on your head. You could have been killed. I'm so sorry. I'm so sorry." Mama was beside herself trying to console me while I lay there with my throbbing head and my aching heart.

"Mama, how about the relay?"

She kept petting me to calm us both down. "The team didn't make it. But don't you even think about that. Close your eyes and get some sleep. The important thing is you, dahlin'." And when my mama called you "dahlin'" in that certain tone of voice, icebergs melted.

There is still a bump on my cranium, a scar reminding me about the things we cannot control. I was crestfallen that the flagpole accident had thwarted my Olympic dreams of swimming with the team my senior year. The pursuit of competitive sports had lost its luster in one, near-fatal blow.

Fate was inviting me to shift my focus from athletics back to music. If nothing else, the Miss Camden pageant conferred confidence on my musical expression by earning the voice scholarship. Beginning to stand on my own two (bare) feet, I chose music to be the caretaker of my heart and soul.

That dedication to excellence attained by rigorous self-discipline and self-regulation had been instilled in me from the get-go. Now in actual, historic Olympia, my bare feet strode on the hallowed earth where those fabled athletes of long ago were trained, athletes whose legends have endured and inspired for millennia.

I may have never made it to the Olympics, but sauntering through the columned palaestra that day in Olympia knocked it out of the park, hand in hand with John, our bellies full of suckling lamb.

# More Odd Luck

JOHN AND I RETURNED TO ATHENS FROM OUR
Peloponnese excursions. After three months on Patmos, we
had acquired a certain facility in our communication skills,
and we looked like walking sunshine. We went back to stay at
Hotel Cleo for our remaining few days. For a fitting finale to
our romantic escapade, we would take the Orient Express for
Paris, where we were to spend a couple of days before flying
back to the States. And we barely had enough money left to
make it happen.

We did some museum hopping in Athens, delighted to discover another exhibit of the Mycenaean gold in the National
Archeological Museum collection. After the museum, we
stopped to buy nuts, intrigued by an unusual window display, floor to ceiling full of un-cracked pistachios. The idea
was incongruous—all of those nuts trapped in their shells like

ungratified desires. We bought a huge bag of them. Cracked, not trapped.

We were strolling along, talking about our adventures over the past several months, and then suddenly, John mused, "What are we going to do with the car? Damn, we can't just leave it here, can we? We've got to come up with something. We could give it away. It's still good for a few more miles, and somebody might benefit from it."

We went to the American Express Office, which was kind of an attraction for folks away from home to hang out, to get money, and to meet and greet. There, we saw a couple of guys we had run into in Athens before. John asked them if they would like to have our car since it was still running, it had full tank of gas, and we were leaving on the train the next day. John gave them the key, and they couldn't believe their luck. Fondly reflecting on how reliable the Beetle had been for us, we were pleased that now, it would be a windfall to others.

It was our last night in the city of wisdom, and we were dying for octopus. We splurged. We found a cozy restaurant amid the maze of streets, and we ate with gusto our favorite Greek dishes from the savory dolmades all the way to the honeyed baklava and everything in between. Stuffed, we climbed to the top of the Acropolis where, on that October evening of starlit indigo, the magic of Athens was unmatched.

We got an early morning start, scrambling to get our bags packed, taking leave with thanks to Cleo and Athens, and we boarded the Orient Express aimed straight for Paris, the city of lights.

We had been looking forward to the return trip, but the Orient Express wasn't like in the movies. It was a bit more faded and decadent. Nonetheless, it was comfy, and John and I settled in for the next leg of our journey. We cozied up, my head on his shoulder. Watching Greece pass by like a landscape watercolor, I dozed off in the lull of love and locomotion. That is, until the train lurched, jarring me into consciousness. "What's going on?"

John said, "No big deal. We're at the Yugoslavian border. We have to get off the train now and go through passport control."

Pulling out our passports, we disembarked the Orient Express to stand in a long line. From here on, my entire perspective of life changed. It was the nature of the situation and the nature of the times.

As a man, John was thrust into the position of being my protector. The Greek customs clerk, holding John's passport, hurled a stream of questions at John, who did his best to reply. Then, opening my passport, the clerk pointed his finger, repeating the same litany of inquiries. I bristled.

John grunted. "We need to gather up our bags and take another train back to Athens."

"Back to Athens? Why?" I asked in disbelief.

"Kathryn, they won't let us leave Greece. It's stamped on our passports that we entered the country in a car, and they won't let us leave until we find the car or pay a shitload of money." John was getting more agitated.

My stomach sank. "What are we going to do?" I asked.

We were ushered into a waiting room of sorts. It looked like a hotel lobby in a spaghetti Western. My fear mounted. A man who spoke English and Greek, and who took an interest in our circumstances, struck up a conversation with us about our predicament. He interpreted the insides of our passports while reminding us that Greece was under the rule of the dictator Papadopoulous. This was learning the hard way for sure.

Truth is stranger than fiction, as the saying goes, and we were right in the midst of a modern-day Agatha Christie mystery. We had to wait till nearly dark when we were herded at last onto the return train for Athens. That punitive train ride was even worse than the deck-class boat ride to Patmos.

First of all, we had no idea where we were going except back to Athens, all but broke. Security led us to a jam-packed train car, and we were lucky to get the last seats before it was standing room only. It smelled terrible. Several women with plain cotton scarves on their heads, their sandaled feet crusty, carried oily packages of food wrapped in brown paper tied in string. There was even one woman who held on her lap a cage—with a rooster in it. This was very different from the Greece that we had known and loved when we were tourists. But even as misfits, we fit right in on a metaphysical level.

After being bounced back to Athens on that overnight train, we were exhausted. With no other idea than to sleep, we went back to Cleo's and took a room again. We thought we had enough money to last a few days, but little did we know, it would be quite a few more than a few. We were skating on thin ice.

My role for now was to defer to John in public. While figuring out what to do next, we went back and recounted our sad tale to Cleo at the hotel. She agreed to let us stay there on credit until we could get things sorted out. Different people advised us in different directions. First we were told to declare the car stolen and report it to the police. After seeing the prison, we thought twice about that.

We got an appointment with the Minister of Justice, who tactfully informed us that our case was not a matter of justice but of Greek law. Then we went to the American Embassy. I thought they would take care of everything for us, being US citizens who had not committed a crime—or, for sure, not an intentional one.

In the American Embassy, the clerk assigned to us was Greek. Ruling from his chair, lording over us in ragged English, all he would say was, "I cannot do anything for you."

John and I had made repeated visits, telling him the same facts each time, almost ready to get on our knees, asking, "Please, it couldn't be that hard to get a copy of the bill of sale from Holland."

That bill of sale would prove the age of the car and the sale price in order for them to assess the appropriate taxes. This vital information was not specified on our passports, and the taxes on a new Bug were astronomical: $12,000.

In the embassy, Americans carrying briefcases came and went. I asked our torturer, "Why can't we see one of *them*?"

He gave some bogus excuse, basically cutting us off at every turn.

John was simmering like Vesuvius, and all this was leading to an angry blow-up.

And then, light bulb: *Why don't we go to the Netherlands Embassy?*

I puffed myself up, looked the revolting reprobate in the eyes for effect, and said, "John and I think we had best leave here and go straight to the Netherlands Embassy. My Van Westervelt blood is boiling over." I can't believe to this day I mustered the gumption to say that out loud.

Pompously, the bureaucrat said, "Why go to the Netherlands Embassy? They are not looking for work. And you are not even Dutch."

We had had enough. John and I turned on our heels as fast as we could toward the Dutch Embassy. The two miles of clogged streets flew by under our feet. At last entering the lobby, we exhaled in tandem. John politely addressed the receptionist in English, and she showed us into the office of Mr. Kuypers.

After the scowling and intimidating Greek clerk at the American Embassy, Mr. Kuypers was truly a breath of fresh air. Order abounded. On the wall behind him was a portrait of Queen Jiuliana of the Netherlands. On his desk was a large vase full of freshly cut, brightly colored tulips. He peered through them with smiling eyes. "How may I help you?" he asked in perfect English.

I swear, the dread and tension evaporated.

John and I relaxed, relaying our saga and how our own embassy had been giving us the runaround for days. We asked

Mr. Kuypers if there was any possibility that he could locate the bill of sale for us. His answer was prompt: "Certainly, we can do that. All we need to do is to contact The Hague. Can you come back in forty-eight hours? We will have your necessary documentation for tax purposes."

I could have cried. He made it look easy to be kind and precise and understanding. In that instant, my Dutch heritage made me proud—it had been a bright idea to call on him. We thanked him profusely, confirming the time for our return. These most valuable documents would assure us that we would "only" need to pay $600 in taxes to the Greek government for a car that we bought for $100. By that time, $600 seemed a stroke of luck. Two days later, as promised, the official, wax-sealed documents from The Hague were in our possession.

Now all we needed was the money. Back in the day when communication wasn't at our fingertips, normal folks traveling in Greece had to reserve well in advance the time for an international call. We reserved our time slots, which entailed waiting for three days before making our calls to the States.

I called home to check in, and what a check-in. My parents had separated. Dad had moved out. My brother and sister, Richard and Susan, had had a motorcycle accident. Sheba, our border collie, had run out in front of the bike on the dirt road. Poor Sheba died, and they were badly injured. Hearing Mama's sad news, I couldn't bring myself to tell her about our troubles, much less ask for money.

When I walked out of the booth, John opened his arms in a hug. Then he called his mother. She had recently divorced his father—what a strange coincidence in both of our families. In spite of what she was going through, his mother didn't hesitate to send him the money to get us home safely.

Totally drained, we walked back to the hotel, sat out on the balcony, and tried to settle our nerves. Cleo stopped by to see how we were doing. Such a generous soul, she brought Greek coffee and fruit. Then John got a call from a diplomatic woman, related to John's brother's wife, who offered to take us to dinner that evening. Maybe the tide had turned and we were out of the worst of it.

After our treat from Cleo, we went to nap in our room. We had been holding on for days since the fated train ride, and now we could see a brighter tomorrow. The moment we had closed our door, we were shedding the world outside as quickly as we shed our clothing. We stood there in our naked honesty. The electricity took charge with a full-body hug that melted our numbness. All the pent-up stress released in orgasm, our breaths slowly subsiding through the sexual aftershocks.

When we woke up, we decided to shower together to save time. This is burned in my memory, the way his knowing touch intimately slathered me with the rich, citrusy shower gel. Afterward, we peeled ourselves away from each other and dried off.

Invited out, we would don our best for the occasion and celebrate. It made me feel good to dress up. I put on my one and only silky mini dress with the red and chartreuse paisley that made my eyes pop.

Aside from the substantial Mediterranean breakfasts providing everything imaginable, farm to table at Cleo's, the rest of our daily meals had only consisted of a scant souvlaki and some pistachios. To save money and our stomachs, we had been ordering meatless souvlakis. That sliced mystery meat was made of god only knows what, and the stench of it....Our mantra was "souvlaki, no meat." Sometimes the server would give us more cucumbers and tomatoes, but even that could get boring for two meals a day.

At dinner, the American woman kindly offered to loan John the money if there were to be any problem with getting it from the States in a timely fashion. In spite of our present difficulties, John and I were still in favor with the gods and goddesses. Cleo, too, was extending credit. And we couldn't forget the kindness of Mr. Kuypers. Our anxiety subsided. We regained some faith in humanity.

The money from John's mother arrived, and we settled our debts, leaving Athens once and for all. By changing our return date, we were rerouted. Now we would fly to Istanbul for two days and Amsterdam for another couple of days until, at last, our trip home to New York.

# Let Me Tell You about Istanbul

LET ME TELL YOU ABOUT ISTANBUL. FROM THE Istanbul airport, John and I took a bus into town, Turkish public transportation being the most affordable means. We boarded the bus and found seats near each other on opposite sides of the aisle. Sitting in the window seat beside me was a middle-aged man scratching his ankle. I tried not to look, but my eyes defied me. I followed his movement and spied a dagger tucked into his sock. It lent a sinister tone to the ride.

The rusty red sun was setting into the Black Sea through a domed silhouette of the exotic skyline. It was transfixing. But when we stepped down from the bus, the first thing we saw were civil guards armed with machine guns.

Continuing to feel out of place in the unlit streets, pressing as close to John as possible, I was unavoidably a six-foot beacon with my long, blond hair flashing in what little light there was. John picked up our pace. People were crowding us. Then someone attempted to trip me right on the street. It was aggressive. I regained my hold on John, and we hurried along.

We had heard that the Pudding Shop was a youth hostel and restaurant centrally located to the Blue Mosque, Hagia Sophia, and the Grand Bazaar. It sounded good since we were counting our pennies every step of the way, and youth hostels back then typically only cost pennies a night. We were grateful to be there, among other Americans, foreign students, and fellow travelers. After scarfing a bowl of the signature rice pudding, we went to our room, and it felt good to lock the door.

"Kathryn, with you on my arm, every man on the streets of Istanbul was following us," John said. "Phew! I need to sit down."

"I know. It was a total nightmare. I was panicking. Thanks for being my bodyguard." I kissed his cheek.

"Well, I hope it's not this bad during the light of day," John said. "Slight change of plans. Let's cram in all the sightseeing we can tomorrow and then go on to the airport. We can crash there. I don't want to stay in this city an extra night."

I nodded wholeheartedly.

Barely fitting into the bed, we crawled under the covers fully clothed. Before long, we heard the sound of the evening ezan chanted from the minaret of the Blue Mosque, broadcast throughout the city. The high-pitched drone wafted in and out of my consciousness.

"Come closer," John murmured. He unzipped my jeans to gently caress me. I could feel his excitement throbbing. "Are you too scared to fuck in Istanbul, Kathryn?" he teased.

By that point, I was beyond words. I unzipped his jeans, too, and we went at it, throwing caution to the wind.

The muezzin's eerie chant woke us early. We pulled ourselves together, packed, and grabbed breakfast. Our big day of touring would start with Istanbul's Grand Bazaar. We walked the old city streets already bounding with life and color, searching for the famous hammered copper pots to take home. We found a vendor in the market with gleaming copperware of every style and shape, from the delicate Turkish coffee urns to sturdy stockpots. We picked two: one sauté pan and one casserole, both with finely crafted brass handles and matching lids. John did the expected haggling, and we got a good deal. That handmade copper would add a touch of class to our supper clubs back home.

The Grand Bazaar was a bizarre whirlwind of humanity, and we didn't linger. Men would drop coins at our feet and bend down and, to our astonishment, blatantly look up my skirt. There were children curved into beasts of burden, carrying heavy oriental carpets on their young backs. We stopped at a kiosk to buy a couple of candy bars. When the vendor gave me back the change, he smacked it firmly in my palm, squeezing so hard I thought my fingers would break. I had to jerk my hand back. In reflection, my ignorance of the world at large and of other cultures was in play. Even though I was in a proper dress and cardigan, I must have appeared strange in their eyes.

John and I were determined, however, to see the rest of the sights. No lollygagging for us. World-famous temples and jewels of untold splendor awaited us.

Our shoes blended in with masses of other pairs beside the door, and we stepped barefoot into the Blue Mosque. There were no places to sit. Walking about speechless, soaking in the tranquil sanctuary, we opened our gaze to exalting space: a flood of stained-glass windows, gigantic chandeliers, minarets on either side of the central dome, thousands upon thousands of blue tiles on the walls, and woven carpets under the knees of the faithful, all patterns and energies pointing to Mecca.

We had entered through the northern door designated for non-worshippers in between prayer times, and we could see the poses of pilgrims praying in the western portion. The mosque was named for the twenty thousand blue Iznik tiles on the walls depicting a myriad of images inspired by the geometry of nature. Toward the top wall of the mosque was a multitude of tiles with elaborate floral designs. On the lower levels were other images from nature like fruits and trees. I went into a trance, yet a conscious one, different from a dream, real and unreal at the same time.

Our day unfolded with one mystery after the next. We progressed to the Hagia Sophia, The Church of the Holy Wisdom, where East and West were intertwined like two praying hands. The emperor Constantine had brought the Christianity of the West to Constantinople, now Istanbul, and he ordered construction of the original church on the site. Under the later rule of Justinian I, the mammoth domed Basilica of today was built. It was a gem of Christian Byzantine architecture complete with marble columns and opulent mosaics. After being looted during the crusades, it was converted into an Islamic Imperial Mosque by Sultan Mehmet II. This august dome now stands as a museum that cups these two expressions of faith.

Topkapi Palace, the former residence of the Ottoman Empire rulers, was close by, and we wanted to see the famous jewels whose alluring drama drew us in to the dimly lit room like a siren song. We marveled at all eighty-six karats of the spectacular Spoonmaker's Diamond. And when we saw the Sultan's emerald-studded dagger, we thought about the movie *Topkapi* and the starring role the dagger played. But more enchanting still was a flamboyant hanging lamp whose solid gold hexagonal frame, pearls dripping from the bottom, capped a giant emerald. The light coming from such a large emerald gave a shimmer of green to the entire room.

After tearing ourselves away from the jewels, we toured the gardens leading to the Imperial Harem, the private quarters of the Sultan, where again the beauty of floral tiles, lush carpets, embroidered cushions, jewel-encrusted candlesticks, and Murano glass was astounding.

John leaned in and said in a low voice, "This is where the royal fucking went on." That said, we skirted the circumcision room and the Court of the Eunuchs on our way back to the Pudding Shop to retrieve our bags and our copper pots. The bus dropped us before dark at the airport, which we thought would be a good place to get away from the persistent broadcasts and menacing people on the streets.

We found a couple of adjacent seats inside the waiting area where it was permissible to hang out until our morning flight to Amsterdam. Even hard airport seats felt more comfortable than downtown Istanbul. We ate some pistachios, settled in for the night, and decided to take turns sleeping to be safe. John was tired, and I took first watch. I had to reassure him every time he drifted off; he would constantly check his hip pocket for his wallet and passport.

We survived that stint in the airport, and other than a few aches and pains, we were ready to board the plane for Amsterdam, thankful to say farewell to Istanbul. But Istanbul wasn't through with us yet. We stood in the line waiting for passport control, and my gut tensed up. In those days, the security check was random. When we were about to get the "all clear," a clerk confiscated our copper pots. I was furious. When I asked why other people were allowed to board the plane with pots like ours, he spitefully shooed us forward, clutching our treasured souvenirs.

"That bastard," John uttered through his teeth. "He stole our pots." We didn't understand about ransom.

Thank goodness the plane ride was short. I was floating from the moment Amsterdam air surrounded me. John said it felt like the "Ritz of Humanity" after Athens and Istanbul.

At the airport office, John picked up a check sent by Kristina's father, who lived in Germany. John was comfortable asking him for a loan since their families were longtime friends. For me, Kristina's shadow was still in the background. John was obviously doing his best to take care of me. He even sold his cherished Nikon camera.

Fate had mercifully brought us back once again to Amsterdam, and with the sale of the camera and Kristina's father's loan, we had enough money to make the rest of our trip easier. We took a room in a little hotel on the canal and flopped into bed.

When we woke up the next day, summer was over. Amsterdam was cold with winter approaching, and we had only summer clothing. We went to the walking district of the city to see what we could find. In the window of a fashionable shop, John pointed out a moss green and heather striped, cowl-necked sweater. I could hardly wait to try it on. It was a great fit, and the vivid, earthy colors were flattering. That sweater would keep me warm during our transition from the end of our European adventures back home to New York, where it would be chilly in every sense of the word.

# Crazy Coincidences

THIS IS NOT A FAIRY-TALE ROMANCE. THIS IS real life, real events, real struggles, real people, and real love. First of all, I wasn't aware at the time that I was pregnant, attributing my heightened sensitivity to the series of challenges that we were going through before and upon our safe return to the States and New York. I had skipped a few periods but had tossed it off to traveling through different time zones and missing a birth control pill or two. My breasts were noticeably becoming tender, my jeans were growing snugger, and my fatigue was inexplicable. It had me wondering.

I had flown from New York to South Carolina to have Thanksgiving dinner with Mama and my brothers and sisters. The normally pleasing holiday smells triggered waves of morning sickness. I kept getting up from the table, pretending to be busy with something other than going to the bathroom to wretch, terrified that anyone would find out.

The day after Thanksgiving, in a meeting with my former psychiatrist and now friend, I asked him if he thought I could be pregnant.

He took one look at me: "Sunshine, yes, I think so, but go to a clinic right away when you get back to New York. It's legal there now to get an abortion if you choose. If it's not already too late." He gave me the name and address of a clinic in Manhattan.

The very thought of telling anyone what was going on or of having an abortion made me cringe. I didn't know which way to turn. After all, we were not married. We had no means of supporting ourselves. We had not even finished college. We were both from Catholic-Episcopal upbringings fraught with guilt. We had begged for money in order to earn our safe passage back to the States from Europe. And now, we were even staying at John's mother's home.

I clearly remember the subway ride to the clinic, utterly alone. And the diagnosis was confirmed. Yes, I was pregnant, but it might be an ectopic pregnancy, and further testing was prescribed. Petrified, how would I tell John…what would I do? What would *we* do?

The long, cold, and hard-driving subway ride back to West Eighty-Ninth Street cruelly propelled me and my dream up the stairs from the street, right through the doorway, literally shattering me. With John's mother watching, I lost the baby on that brownstone floor.

John's mother took care of me and sought good medical attention. I bounced back. At least, that was an illusion I held dear while willing the loss to recede into the background, carrying on with my youthful optimism as if nothing had happened. My dysfunctional childhood programmed my denial.

Even though John's father had moved out due to the divorce, he was instrumental in my landing a job, a "holiday extra" in the upscale women's department of Lord and Taylor on Fifth Avenue. It sounds more glamorous than it was. And John got his license to be an NYC taxi driver.

We were struggling to survive. Getting a toehold in Manhattan was proving to be out of our league. We thought our future could be better if we packed up and returned to finish our degrees. Coming back on the college scene was a jolt after Europe and New York. I enrolled again to study voice; and as before, the instructor pushed me toward being a soprano, which was wrong for me. The drug and booze scene all over campus was wrong for me, too. Nothing was working, and life was all at odds.

# Expressions

ONE DAY IN THE FINE ARTS BUILDING AT USC, I heard the most glorious music coming from the rehearsal room down the hall. I followed it like a mouse to cheese. There was a beautiful woman playing Bach on the classical guitar. I stood there and listened. It opened to me a realm of undreamed possibilities wanting to be able to do what she did. It had made me angry when these teachers didn't understand what to do with my young contralto voice.

Therefore, a good plan B was to wrap myself around the guitar and invite the muse. I decided to study with that woman, who turned out to be the guitar professor. She encouraged me. I practiced for hours on end. John loved hearing the metronome mark time; and etudes, scales, and arpeggios filled the walls of our apartment near campus.

I didn't trust the pill any longer, and the doctors recommended the IUD for birth control, a common practice of female torture of the day. It sucked. Making love with John became uncomfortable and, then, even painful. John said he could feel the IUD when he was inside me, which freaked me out, too. It was impossibly awkward to talk about it, even to my doctor.

All of that made my interest in sex wane. Instead, I hung out with friends and fellow music students, focusing more on my studies. John and I drifted apart, our intimacy ebbed, and neither of us could get a grip on it. My fear of not being good enough dominated me. I still compared myself to Kristina. The thought that he might still be in love with her hounded me. Why hadn't he asked me to marry him? That insecurity gnawed at me.

John and a friend and I drove out to the Grand Tetons where they would work a summer job for three months at the national park. Flying back after only a few weeks in order to make summer school, I hit my studies hard. By the time John returned from his park job in Wyoming, our relationship was fragmenting.

The breakup was excruciating. My conclusion was either I have no life purpose at all or my purpose was beyond my imaginings and could only be uncovered through doing it.

It was my own drive that had pushed me out the door. Making a total commitment to my music studies gave me something meaningful to sink my teeth into, and I held on to it like a dog with a bone. Music was the place for all of my feelings about failing to have John's child, about failing to measure up to Kristina, about failing to somehow prevent my parents from divorcing.

My first memory of the muse visiting me: I was six years old, chosen to sing in the Gregorian chant choir at my school. When my best friend's father died, my choir was invited to sing the Requiem Mass at his funeral. My sadness for my friend conflicted with my delight in getting to sing the Mass. Clearly, the muse was stronger than guilt.

The main constant in my life was music of one kind or the other. My first instrument in the school band was the flute, and my parents insisted that I stick with it, but I had other ideas. All of the neighborhood kids were playing guitars, and I loved the songs of the sixties and wanted to sing them. I snuck off to a pawn shop to trade my flute for my first guitar. This upset my parents especially because it involved hanging out with musical activists and the "in crowd." I sat on my bed with that Joan Baez songbook and mastered every song.

At USC, learning to visualize clearly and to organize my mind became my haven of sanity from the sex, drugs, and rock and roll craziness all around me. The joy of music slowly repaired my self-esteem. My mantra was more like peace, love, and rock and roll. (Or Bach and roll.)

My guitar professor and woman role model suggested that I audition in Baltimore with the esteemed pedagogue Aaron Shearer at Peabody Conservatory. With only one year's study of the classical guitar, I'm amazed to this day at my daring, my conviction, and my resultant achievement.

What a cherished moment, playing for Shearer. He could have been harsh, but instead, he gave me a real music lesson by telling me that while I wasn't technically proficient enough to compete in the conservatory, I possessed something he wished more of his students had—something that could not be taught—innate musicality. "There is a place in music for everyone," he told me, "and you will find yours." Shearer agreed to let me take his repertory and pedagogy classes. This was the beginning of a student-teacher relationship and friendship lasting until his death.

My emotional state was in high gear when I returned to Columbia. The successful audition meant I would need to move up to Maryland. I hated to hurt John, but if I stayed, I would resent him. If I left, I would lose him in a different way. Duke Ellington said, "Music is my mistress, and she don't play second fiddle to no one."

In Baltimore, I met a guy. We had the same guitar teacher. One day after class, he invited me to his apartment and offered me some sweet tea. His mother was from Tennessee, and he told me he liked my Southern accent. He put on some Hendrix, and it didn't take long. We went into the bedroom and had sex; and immediately, he wanted me to move in with him.

After the miscarriage with John, my mistaken thinking had gone something like this: if I was going to have another sexual relationship, it was better to have a commitment of marriage. But in no time at all, his infidelities incensed me, and he tried to thwart my studies by diminishing me. The marriage came and went within a year's time. I finally got rid of the IUD and husband number one.

I moved back to Columbia and graduated from USC. I had been saving money working my part-time job in a popular head shop where I met the poet Iris. We plotted an adventure, both being recently divorced. At first, I went to Rome while Iris went to Paris. We met up on the Italian island of Ischia for the summer, where I had booked a gig at a resort hotel singing in the cantina.

This was the "have guitar, will travel," a.k.a., *la dolce vita* phase of my life. I even went to the Greek island of Ithaca. Every time I smelled the salty spray and tasted the unforgettable foods, memories of John flooded my consciousness. Even though I was on a different island, in my mind, I was transported to Patmos and John. I wondered what he was doing now, how he was, where he was. All of the "water under the bridge" vanished in my daydreams.

While in Italy, I attracted exotic lovers and exotic experiences. I fell into the jazz music ex-pat scene in Rome, where I mingled with all sorts of people, making friends easily. One night, I went to a famous movie producer's villa with one of my lovers, an aspiring actor and a young aristocrat in exile from Afghanistan. The party took place on a grand rooftop overlooking the pool and gardens. Bored with the social hobnobbing, we decided to take off our clothes and dance carefree under the bright moonlight; no one even noticed. And there was no one casting a shadow of blame. The natural extension of this led me to further explore my sensuality with several women, friends, and strangers in various combinations.

# Control Release

AND THEN, I CAME HOME TO MAMA'S IN MOBILE, Alabama. It was like getting sucked into a cultural ghetto. A boyfriend I had met in Oxford, England, came to visit me. Everyone was trying to set him up with my younger cousins while pointedly ignoring me. He was ten years younger than I was, and that horrified my family in the typical Southern fashion.

There were not a lot of jobs around Mobile for someone with a bachelor's degree in music. I found one delivering singing telegrams in eye-catching, special occasion, costume regalia, and I even worked as a travel agent—a traditional job. I tried to be normal. Control.

Release…I had an affair with an acquaintance. A Jesuit priest, no less. He showed up on my doorstep in the middle of the night—he needed to talk to me. He was brilliant, lusty, appealing, and drunk. He seduced me. I thought it was the real thing, but it wasn't. He wound up leaving the priesthood and marrying someone else.

A cosmopolitan, educated, dynamic woman alone in the deep South spelled trouble. Here a tall blonde was not that unusual, but one with a clue was. The small-town atmosphere smothered me.

One divorce down, a few trips to Europe, some flings there and here, and then I met my second husband. Gutted and mortified after breaking off the relationship with the priest, I needed to try once again to be normal by conforming to some kind of order to make me less vulnerable. Control.

I tried to be a conventional wife. He was witty yet a brooding intellectual. I was more attracted by his mind than any physical attributes, which played out in the bedroom. After we married, his affection cooled. He was terrified that I would get pregnant. He lugubriously ranted and raved that he didn't want children. A gifted organist, he told me, "We would either have a Mozart or a monster. Someday you'll thank me for not giving you my child." (And I do.)

At the end of the 1980s, with the first Gulf War impending, his paranoia increased, and he stockpiled guns and ammo while combining alcohol and psychiatric drugs indiscriminately. When he started sleeping with a loaded pistol at the head of the bed, the walls of our home resonated with angst instead of music.

One night, I went with friends to hear the Charlotte Opera Production of *The Merry Widow*. I saw my unhappiness on the head of a pin, and I cried the entire opera. I faced the fact that my eleven-year marriage was over.

I moved out and found a rooming house. It was a bitter, cold Christmas, yet I still had to act cheerful at my holiday gigs. My cramped space forced me to pile shoeboxes and other belongings on top of the refrigerator. The couple in the adjoining room banged out-loud sex every night. It was all too close for comfort. Full-tilt therapy was required.

I had tried on the mold of conventional marriage twice, and twice I'd had to shake it off. This must mean I could not be a conventional wife. Therapy showed me how to examine what I was doing to repeat such unsuitable patterns for myself and for others.

My goal was to make a future for myself, to be independent and self-supporting—not easy to do in the pervasive culture. Teaching at two universities, with a choir soloist job along with various music gigs around town, I was barely keeping my head above water financially. I set my course for a Master of Music Performance degree, which steered me toward more job security and the path to tenure.

We had been staying somewhat in touch after the time that John called me in Charlotte, working his ninth step. While he was living in St. Louis, he had sent me pictures of his two, precious, towheaded sons. He sounded happy, and I was happy for him. But I wasn't truly happy for myself.

It never stopped until the hormones slowed down, my wanting to have children. Women who have children sometimes wonder what their lives would be like without children. And women without children wonder what it would be like to have a child. I did wonder. And I always thought I would eventually have a child. Timing and relationships didn't jive, but even that didn't dampen my maternal instincts. I nurtured my family, friends, cats, dogs, students, and I babied my guitar. But honestly, I didn't know how to nurture myself.

On a more positive note, my teaching position at Queens College, now Queens University of Charlotte, was very rewarding. It afforded me endless opportunities to perform. To top it off, my students were hardworking and inspiring. My recognition in the arts community expanded as a result of my dedication both as a performer and an educator.

I did the Jungian dream work and journaled to empower myself as a single woman. Confronting my nightmares made them retreat. Meditation practice put peace within reach. I was dating, but it was nothing serious. Marriage was the furthest thing from my mind.

Then, I met my third husband. He had a European flair, and he was a solid person in both career and attitude. He brought me flowers and expensive perfume, and he wined and dined me as only an attractive Italian man can. A breath of fresh air, he was a fifty-year-old bachelor who wasn't interested in having children. By that time, neither was I. We had fun, and we could talk openly about sex. We had a healthy relationship that wasn't codependent. When his work called him back to Milan, he wanted me to go with him. I refused to leave my job for a love affair. He proposed. I left Charlotte and moved to Milan as his wife.

Italy was not the same for a resident as for a tourist. Homesickness got to me to the point that one day, I called the long-distance operator just to hear an American accent. Sightseeing and full cultural immersion for three years kept me busy. During that time, I wrote and published two music books: *The Guitar Songbook for Music Therapy* and my arrangements of *Six Neapolitan Songs for the Classic Guitar*.

I pleaded with my husband to apply for an assignment that would get us back to the US, and he picked one in New York. However, in Poughkeepsie, New York, nothing changed except the language. An icy and snow-bound winter and a husband who was never there compelled me to move back south. One time when he was halfway around the world on business, there was a whiteout in New York when all I had to shovel myself out with was a broom and a dustpan. That was it for me. I told him, "My dear, you have to live here, and I don't." Our marriage was on shaky ground.

Mama found a condo for me in Fairhope, Alabama. She was glad to be close by. Shortly thereafter, my husband got cancer. I urged him to come down to Alabama for the surgery, where my physician cousins could make sure he received the best care. Mama was right there with us all the way. My husband promised that if he made it through the cancer, he would make life changes. We gave it our best.

*Soul*

I HAD GOTTEN TO THE END OF ACADEMIA AND classical music. Playing Bach and singing Ravel were replaced by singing my own songs at Nashville's Bluebird Café, at the Ernest Tubb Midnight Jamboree, and in jazz clubs. And now, I had gotten to the end of my third marriage.

I never had a white-dress wedding, and my husbands never wanted children. The breakup with John was even more painful than my three divorces. This left me wondering what it all meant.

Now, when John and I reflect on our time together as young lovers, neither of us can remember the specifics of our breakup. We each have our version. It's an emotional blur, unlike the intricate details we remember in all other aspects of our history.

After John and I split up, a bleak loneliness overwhelmed me, yet I was able to tuck my feelings deep inside. The optimism of youth is confusing. As usual, I had carried on, believing

I would find again what I had lost. And throughout my life, touches of the divine danced through my body, mind, heart, and soul. I would give and give, and hope and hope, and love and love. I could always tell the muse, and she would understand me. And there had always been Mama, who got me no matter what.

This understanding was dawning on me when Mama died, and I realized I had lost my original soul mate. And it was only then that all other relationships of love, no matter how full of heart, were inexpressibly lacking. There was that loneliness again.

But after losing Mama, the loneliness became unbearable: that lack of epic connection with the womb. While I grieved, husband, family, and friends helpfully tried to be there for me, but it wasn't working. And I tried to explain. I called my therapist. I made mistakes. I stopped feeling lighthearted.

In that first visit with John, my heart knew what my head needed time to learn. Being with him satisfied a longing I had not identified, and across what seemed eons, a connection was instantly renewed. That archetypal union the poets and the prophets extol. Synchronicity: Jung held that coincidences are related evocatively as a result of universal forces.

It wasn't until John and I reconnected forty-seven years later that I would understand what had been going on. How I had gotten from there to here. And what bliss it would be to be with him again, to be whole again, to be his, and for him to be mine. A soul mate equals unconditional love. And John had made his promise good to Mama after all.

# *Priorities*

PRIORITIES, PRIORITIES: THAT'S WHAT SHEARER emphasized. Once, in an argument with a movement educator about the priorities of the performing artist, I challenged his position that we only perform to fill and to fulfill our own shortcomings. I declared that it is possible to perform out of sheer joy. Isn't the artist knee-deep in there working to bring order and beauty to it all?

Shearer, the great guitar pedagogue and mentor for most of my adult life, ultimately slowed down. Hospice was attending him; he had stopped eating. He asked me, "What's that song…?" and started to sing, "The way you wear your hat…" (Gershwin's "They Can't Take That Away from Me"). I joined in, heart in my throat.

I asked him tenderly if he had any final words of wisdom for me. He said that priorities define our relationship with life and art. In a voice barely audible but convincing, he added, "Love as much as you can. That's all."

Relationships may be rooted in the truth and the full expression of joy. They do not need to be places to hide. Love is the light of the soul. Creativity is the spiritual force. It is the alchemy transforming negative thinking into positive action. It has given me a path to follow and songs to sing. And life is the big stage. You wear your ego front and center when you walk on that stage to shine. And when you walk off the stage, you put your ego back in its place, and you shine from the inside out.

And the beat goes on. The manifestations of an artistic life, I've poured that into boxes of journals, foreign language fluency, students molded for careers, songs sung and heard in various venues, seven published CDs, and three books.

It's important for us women to list our accomplishments without apology. For a woman of a certain age, finding true love is an added benefit, or a lagniappe, of a life lived well. Even though the garage is full of boxes of my *Desperate Diva* CDs today, this much is true: in the words of the uncompromising optimist Julian of Norwich, in her *Showing: Revelations of Divine Love* (c. 1395), the first book known to have been written by a woman in the English language: "All shall be well, all shall be well, and all manner of thing shall be well."

# Jazz

A PINK LIGHT BLOOMS, SOFTENING THE MARSH grasses. The palmetto tree and the live oak are waking up, too. I hear John grinding the beans to prepare the elixir of life. The air is filled with the spicy aroma of magical sweet potato muffins. Small as it may be, our kitchen is the heart of the house, and our "supper club" now serves breakfast, lunch, dinner, and high tea.

"Here you are, sweetness," John says in a near whisper.

I prop myself up on the pillows to receive his morning offering. "Thank you, baby," are the first words I utter, cradling the hot cup and lifting it to my lips.

After a few quiet sips, in mock seriousness, John asks me, "Do you see the bunny out there?"

I peer out over the tidal marsh and see an upright piece of driftwood rising from the reeds. "You mean over there? That does look like a bunny," I reply.

"White light on the bunny's ears," John says. "It's going to be a full bunny day."

I play along. "Hmm…I can't see anything but ears yet. The rest is still in the shadows. Those lines of light make it look striped like the tiger."

"Won't be long now," says John. "It probably needs more coffee."

A bit of a breeze touches the marsh grasses like a jazz drummer's brush roll.

John cheerfully baritones, "*Break forth, oh beauteous heavenly light, and usher in the morning.*"

I chime in, and we fumble through the lyrics to sing the last refrain together, "*Our peace eternal making.*"

"Do you think the bunny could hear us?" I ask.

"Sure, it could, lovey. It doesn't miss much," he reassures me, re-fluffing the pillows, continuing to sing, this time his own thoughts shaping into instant song:

"*Beaufort tomatoes, they taste so fine,*
*They're better than merlot wine.*"

And by this time, our toes are flirting, tapping out John's rhythm:

"*Raised in the sunshine next to the sea,*
*It's the kind of place that you would love to be,*
*Yeah, Beaufort tomatoes, mmm, so great.*"

John growls and snuggles up to me.

"*Put some Beaufort tomatoes on my plate.*"

Smiling, slurping coffee, and staring at the bunny now in full sunlight, I sink into the bed. "The bunny is up, but I'm going under cover."

John wraps himself around me and starts making circles on my belly. "This is the omphalos of the world where all life began. I want to put peach marmalade in your bellybutton and top it with one single blueberry."

"But what would the bunny say about that?" I play along.

The banter continues in the arena of the absurd, and soon we're doubled over. When I watch him laugh, I can't help but laugh harder.

"Full-tilt bunny," John says. "Look at it, ready for action. Thumper. Thumper. Thump."

"Oh yeah, there it is, up and ready," I snicker. "Good thing we're not on reality TV right now, or they would carry us away. Maybe even order a lobotomy for two. Is there more coffee?" I ask.

"But what about the bunny? It counts on us," John replies in earnest, and he takes another sip.

"I'm not sure. I don't think we should abandon it." And then a striking thought: "John...I mean...what if we're not looking at the same bunny?"

"That's okay, sweetness. It doesn't matter at all."

I see our "marsh bunny" as the personification of our inner children, the kids we are at heart and that we never stopped being: in love with imagination and the dance. We didn't want to be normal anyway. We just wanted to be together.

# Part Two

## JOHN HEYWARD DOWDNEY

# Anticipation

EXHILARATION ECHOED IN THE AIR AND RESO-
nated in my head. Forty-seven years. And now, she was coming
to see me. A terrifying and joyful feeling at the same time. I
reflected on her beautiful, lithe body sitting on the sand in
Macedonia. She eagerly ate a white peach, the juice dribbling
between her breasts onto her abdomen only to be stopped by
the elastic band of her sea-blue string bikini.

For a moment, fear riddled me: Was I worthy? Would she
vanish into the ether again? Ripe peaches and young lovers on
a Macedonian beach. Seasoned by life's experiences, we had
matured, too. First item on the grocery list: peaches, white
peaches.

Memories, dreams, and ruminations resurfaced. Kathryn
was my mythic soul mate. I had been crazy in love with her.
What hadn't been apparent to me at the time was that my

ability to love her had been limited by my addiction. Thirty years in recovery. Maybe this time, honest feelings would govern me rather than mouthing the next line in the script.

When I last saw her, my descent into alcoholism was taking over. She was following her muse, and I was following my genetic propensity and social training from New York City and East Hampton. What's Humphrey Bogart's famous expression? "The problem with the world is that everybody is a few drinks behind." I chose to go into the alcohol rehab center: old-school, hard-core, Midwestern, twelve-step program.

In recovery, I had called Kathryn to make amends while working the ninth step. My amends involved my alcoholic behavior with her after we'd separated due to an unsuccessful attempt to orchestrate a *ménage à trois* before she was to leave town. My desire for lustful sex had replaced caring intimacy. I had walked into the china shop and had broken everything. At twenty-one years old, I had become the person I'd sworn I would never be: Dad.

Making amends with Kathryn, I explained the recovery process of the twelve steps, admitted my behavior was wrong, and determined to do anything to rectify it.

Kathryn's voice was as calm and serene as an angel's. "I hardly remember that instance. I only remember the beautiful things in our relationship. I loved you so much."

I thanked her profusely, got off the phone, and sobbed. Kathryn sounded like tenderness and mercy, a person filled with unconditional love. I had been the problem, and now, with my newly discovered sobriety, I could be the solution.

Time warp: I saw myself in our college apartment, in an upholstered chair with our cat, Tiger, perched on the arm of it. Kathryn was playing classical guitar and using her new footstool. She was proud of it, and it would allow her to hold the classical guitar in the correct position. That day, she was practicing what I thought was a beautiful piece of music, which she told me was an exercise, a Guiliani progression. Her fingers, like spider's legs walking up and down the neck of the guitar, were a vision of precision and beauty. It was the music of the spheres.

God, I had loved her. Kathryn was perfect. She was beautiful. She was smart. She was an artist in the kitchen. She was an artist with the guitar. She was an artist with her voice. And when she took off her clothes, it was the alpha and the omega.

We were mildly crazy and horribly dysfunctional. For the two years that we were together in college, it was "turn on, tune in, drop out." We did it all. We had held on to each other like lifelines on a sailboat in heavy seas. Kathryn was looking to get out of the heavy weather, and I was focused solely on holding on to her, smothering the relationship. The fire went out. There was no oxygen. Direction, motivation, clarity, and inspiration were missing. Fear navigated the vessel of my ego.

By encouraging her to follow her muse even if she left because of it, it wouldn't be my fault. She did, and that was our parting. Drinking took on new meaning, displacing the pain of lost love. Escaping self-examination provided no relief. There's that famous scene in *On the Waterfront*, Brando talking to his brother: "I could have been a contender." Poor me, poor me, pour me another one.

The night we first made love in college, we held hands, fingers intermeshed, electrons flowing, galvanic sensitivity they call it. Looking in her eyes transported me through the far reaches of the galaxy. I was not going to treat her as my father had treated my mother; I was going to have a perfect relationship. Such young and foolish thoughts go with the passion of youth.

There were many birthday emails sent to her over the years, a short note to say that she was an incredibly special person in my life. For example, "Happy birthday—July 3, as I recall. Almost a firecracker. Well, I think that's an understatement. I hope you have a beautiful birthday and a fabulous year. Warmest thoughts and love, John." Keeping it simple avoided the impression of hitting on her. She was happily married. It was important for me to continue thanking her for the two unforgettable years we had spent together. Just a smidge of wisdom and a truckload of faith and gratitude.

Sixty-seven years old, twice divorced, father of two fine sons, grandfather as well, and about to see the woman I had majored in in college—with no idea of what to expect. My disastrous track record in relationships was nil. There were probably some awards for participation, but no ribbons or trophies unless you considered canceled settlement checks to be awards.

I was poorer than a church mouse, having completed the first year of my life alone. No wife, no romance, no girlfriends, no roommates, no children, and no dogs. No car—just a bike. A modest brick cottage overlooking a tidal estuary and marsh-lands near Charleston, South Carolina. Living on the line.

Between the fresh water and the salt sea, between the tidal grasses and the maritime forest, between madness and sanity—only topographical elevation keeping me from becoming primordial ooze.

Kaleidoscopic flashbacks: She told me in one of our conversations after the amends call and after the Twin Towers fell that she was in the middle of her Nashville career. Her dialogue had some of those voguish business expressions: focused objectives, return on equity, kick ass and take names. Had Kathryn devolved into a corporate automaton? The unknowns flew up like witches' brooms on Halloween. Had she become a Walmart Waddler? Did her face have lines like an interstate map? Had some malignant tumor been removed from her body, leaving a concave space? Was she going to be a Xanax zombie popping pills or drinking like a fish? Was she happy?

My guide was the amends call thirty years ago. No expectations. I was going to treat her with the love and kindness she had given me. I was going to be myself. Forty-seven years of additional life experience, thirty-plus years of sobriety, and five years tutelage by Frank, the Buddhist cabdriver in San Francisco.

The invitation to Kathryn had always included her husband. He would probably wind up being an extraordinary human with depth of soul. After all, he had loved her for over twenty years. Had successfully juggled a thousand ideas at a time with Kathryn. He was an Italian who had spent his entire business career with Big Blue. As a naval cadet, he crewed a Tall Ship (ships of wood and men of steel) and toured in submarines as an engineer. Early on, she let me know that he would not be making the trip with her—family business in Italy. Without her husband, the possible perception of impropriety soared. I had no overwhelming desire to get double tapped in the head by someone's Italian second cousin once removed.

Although my amends had been made to her on the phone over thirty years ago, the memories had carried me through many challenging and depressing moments of life. More important, it would be mind-blowing to see how she had evolved from that girl I'd known those many years ago in college.

*On August 16, 2016, at 8:07 a.m., KathrynScheldt1@ getmail.com wrote*:

Subj: Soon to be southbound

Ciao, John, it's been quite a week with the intense heat. Dad and I have survived thanks to A/C, tomato sandwiches, indoor pool, storytelling, and the Olympics. I plan to leave bright and early in the morning and point south. I'm sure to be "rode hard and put up wet" by the time I reach you.

Looking forward to it all. Hugs, K

*On August 16, 2016, at 8:12 a.m., JohnDowdney1@getmail.com wrote*:

Well, if you arrive rode hard and put up wet, you will be beautiful nonetheless. It's an inside thing, as you know. Looking forward to your arrival and presence. Hugs, John

## Arrival

KATHRYN CALLED TWICE AFTER SHE HAD PASSED Pedro's South of the Border. She reported that the miles of traffic had come to a halt on the Pee Dee River Bridge. It was miserably hot. Over a hundred degrees in the shade, and the humidity was not far behind. Lowering the thermostat for the A/C to better refresh her was financial splurging on electrons; for everyone else, it was just civilized.

Most of the blinds were drawn to minimize the sun's effect on the internal house temp. Lifting some slats, looking occasionally for a car that might hold a treasured occupant, I surveyed the few moving cars on the block. A car stopped mid street and did a U-turn. Bingo, that's her? The car slowly passed. The driver had blond hair and a red blouse like the one Kathryn had in college, and that's where the likeness stopped at seven miles an hour.

A multi-reflected splatter of light caught my eye as a baby Benz motored down the street. I went back inside to wait.

A colorfully braceleted wrist came into my view through the glass panel beside my front door. Those magnificently musculatured fingers that could walk up and down a guitar neck like a crab on coke reached out to ring the bell. Already moving, I opened the door, and in the few seconds before eye contact, my expectations went wild. I had to get it together.

Kathryn's white linen suit framed her summer face and blond beach hair. Two terrific red lips glistened. We hugged. Cheek kisses, and a quick one in the middle. Holding her shoulders, examining her face, not in the manner of a surgeon but rather a spiritual friend, I saw her jaw line was strong. As always, her eyes, magnificent eyes, said, *I'm crazy and full of zest for life;* and her body said, *I create with rhythm, melody, and voice.* Time had been very gentle with all of her physical attributes. The lean and lithe Southern girl possessed the remnants of Lolita-esque allure. She had the feminine carriage of an aristocrat: precise, distinct, superior. Yet her movement, whether walking, turning, or reaching, suggested cat, big cat. Smooth, subtle, and incredibly strong. She was purrfect.

I was eager to be the gentleman and spoil her with decorous behavior. When we got the rest of her stuff from her car, she made a big deal about how embarrassed she was that her packing was chaotic. For me, one just had to realize that the automobile was the suitcase. Was there a high level of organization in this suitcase? No, but that was unrealistic, considering she had been on the road for a couple of weeks.

Her back was to me, and she popped open the trunk to retrieve several items. Looking at her as she bent over, I bet her legs were long enough to make it to Savannah. The white linen pants magnified those legs for days. Her ass was pretty much the same perfect size as it had been in college. Her lace underwear peeked through the wrinkles in the linen, reminding me that this was the real thing. No polyester princess here. Real linen, real woman. *Oops, I'm on the wrong track. This is a celibate celebration of friendship.* But God, her bottom looked amazing.

Etiquette and desire focused me to get Kathryn comfortable after her ten hours on the road. She handed me a suitcase, a garment bag, and treats to bring inside. Foodstuffs arrived in a variety of bags and containers. Together, we were putting items away like dancers with new partners, both discovering themselves through their partner's space. Goat's milk, sheep cheese, rice pasta, gluten free. And her complexion was that of a thirty-year-old. I was not going to argue with success.

Next, we got to the Amish farm vegetables. The genes of karmic tomato lovers became apparent. Eight pounds. Fire engine red, burgundy, purple with white fractals, a smell that permeated the kitchen while she talked about the heirloom or cultivar at her fingers' length. And peeking through the paper bag, peaches—white peaches. Kathryn placed them on the counter next to the white peaches I had purchased.

"Do you remember the white peaches of Macedonia?" Kathryn's smile was soft and subtle.

*I wouldn't be the person I am today if I didn't.* "Yes," I said.

The warehouse of my mind shifted to Molly in *Ulysses*: "…I put my arms around him yes and drew him down to me so he could feel my breasts all perfume yes and his heart was going like mad and yes I said yes I will Yes…"

Food requiring refrigeration was refrigerated, and luggage was strategically positioned on the floor for easy access. It all fostered an aura of informality, a harbinger of our journey, and I said, "Come take a look at my garden, Kathryn. It's the gem of the house."

The camellias and azaleas surrounded live oaks and pines of the Southern maritime forest. We glided through garden experiences and horticultural insights—sometimes in line, sometimes abreast—the commencement, unbeknownst to either of us, of weaving a tapestry of the heart.

The hot August day gave way to the hazy twilight with mosquitoes. The perspiration on our brows suggested we retreat inside. It was time for something cool. It was time for the humidity of doubt to be removed.

Taking her bag, I led her to the room with the marsh view and prepared a couple of fizzy waters with lime while Kathryn freshened up from the drive. She opted to sit in one of the Hitchcock chairs in such a way as to indicate a consciousness, centered and balanced. Her eyes inquired. Looking supremely comfortable, she didn't say a word.

I broke the silence, "Kathryn, tell me about your last forty-seven years."

"My first marriage was ridiculously short. It really shouldn't count." Both of her eyes were tracking both of my eyes, and me.

Hubby number one was a musician, he was good-looking, they were young, and it seemed like the right thing to do, da da da da da. Her eyes said, *Fuckup, a total fuckup*. And for a moment, I worried that she might be thinking the same thing about me.

The more we delved into our lives and stories about the evolution of our hearts and souls, the more we discovered we were not reciting merely a chronology of events. She told me what her part had been in the failed marriage. She hadn't been a victim. She took responsibility for her actions or lack thereof. We discovered elements of synchronicity, and an enhanced awareness settled upon us.

It thrilled me that Kathryn didn't shy away from being human, imperfect, and making mistakes. That was part and parcel of what was looking at me now. She had continued to play her own music throughout. She had grown up. And she was still so goddamn beautiful.

After a brief first marriage, she stayed with music: some teaching, gigs in Europe, and the lifestyle of an ex-pat. Next, her free spirit brought her back home to the South to study and to finish her master's. Past lovers of significance got an honorable mention in *My Life as a Free Spirit*, and others, a small piece of joy in her heart with attendant silence.

The level of honesty with which she, possessing an elegant humility, illustrated her tales had no artifice to enhance impact. No apostrophes for creative sequencing. No "how great I am" choruses. No "look carefully at my five thousand successes." On the contrary, a simple, almost Buddhist-like "what you see is what you get."

Raised by alcoholics, I learned to appreciate the architectural complexity in denial, artifice, and rationalization. Here in front of me was a person of deep, spiritual integrity. Her poise and clarity were extraordinary.

"Marriage two was more the norm," Kathryn said. Wonderful in the early years followed by the standard disintegration. They grew apart. "That's the guy I was married to when you called me to make amends," she said. Kathryn turned her chair to face me and said, "Come hold my hands. I need to tell you something."

The intensity of her expression lent seriousness to the dialogue as if she were bracing herself to whisper about death. I moved my chair to face her, and before re-seating, another dose of adrenalin shot through me. Once my fanny hit the cushion, I had donned my suit of invisible armor. Yes, my past behavior had been horrible, and the downward spiral it had taken was epic.

Now, here she was in my living room forty-seven years after our breakup. Psychologically, I was prepared to take the blow, and more importantly, I was determined to think before reacting. Nanoseconds passed like hours. I completed a reflective spectral analysis on her bracelets in the moment before she spoke. Her eyes pierced me. *Oh, shit, this is going to be heavy.*

Kathryn brought my hands together, raised them to her lips, and kissed them. "You need to understand this, John. I have always been wildly in love with you. You are my soul mate. I left because I never thought you would get over Kristina. I had to follow the music to escape the pandemonium."

My thoughts grasped at and for anything familiar. The high-speed films of nuclear detonation before the big flash seemed apropos—the shock wave was coming. Yet nothing was destroyed by the shock wave of love except denial, rationalization, and despair. I wept profusely, and then, I wept again.

# John's Story

A STATE OF FEAR PERVADED MY THOUGHTS AS A child growing up in New York City. In our home, there were fights, and sometimes, blood was drawn. Wrapping myself around my father's leg did nothing to slow him down when he was attacking my mother or my older brother.

At age four, I overdosed on baby aspirin; and two years later, a tonsillectomy left me unable to speak without stuttering. My first solution was to sing tunes from recordings of Broadway shows my parents had attended. If I wanted a peanut butter sandwich, Mom would hear me singing, asking her by putting my words to, say, some Rex Harrison song from *My Fair Lady*. It wasn't elegant or sophisticated, but it got me fed.

Stuttering was worse than a skin color difference in the Anglo-white "Amerika" of the fifties. To me, answering a phone (pre-caller ID) was akin to showering at the Bates Motel.

Others would notice brown skin, even at a distance. A stutterer isn't discovered until he speaks. Many people laugh at stutterers, and right in their faces. And people picked on me. Fights ensued. Children can be cruel. Shit, even my father laughed at me. It was bludgeoned into me that I was different, "a veritable genetic defective."

Kindergarten to third grade entailed speech therapy classes where I always sang instead of speaking. During this time, when it was a trusted person, like from my tight circle of friends, I didn't stutter. But I continued to stutter at home.

Mother told me tales about Demosthenes. He was a fourth-century Greek orator who put pebbles in his mouth to give speeches to the ocean in order to overcome his stuttering. On weekends in East Hampton, I would ride my bike to the beach and imitate Demosthenes.

My speech impediment was an indicator that there were some issues, but it was not the only impediment. Math class afforded new dimensions of expression of that. It was some time in grade school when the travel problem presented itself. "Bob and Sally are traveling from Phoenix to Dallas. The total distance is x miles if they travel four hours at 65 miles per hour. What speed do they need to travel to reach Dallas in x hours?" I examined the problem, and it was clear that there was not enough information to calculate an answer. The teacher's remark was, "See me after class."

I explained to the teacher that the time of arrival or speed could not be determined for several reasons. What time do the liquor stores open, do we have to pass through dry counties, and will Sally be a real bitch that day? With sincerity, I emphasized how each of the variables was significant. He advised me not to introduce variables that weren't in the initial problem. And to top it off, he told me that other classmates had it far worse at home.

More therapy ensued. Be it psychiatrist, psychologist, or counselor, everybody seemed to be focused on getting information that would nail Dad. I couldn't let that happen. We might all wind up in the poorhouse. My job was to keep the family together. A complaint was filed by some of our neighbors, and Dad had counseled me how to answer any interrogation by Child Social Services in case his attorney or political friends could not prevent an intervention. This made me a nervous wreck.

That same year, as Christmas was approaching, inebriated Dad asked me to climb into his lap and tell him what I wanted for Christmas.

"A happy family."

Dad picked me up with both arms and tossed me across the living room. He hollered at my mother, "You've brainwashed the little bastard!"

There was another side to Father: charismatic, bon vivant, with a seemingly unending vitality. To see him half lit, breaking into a Cossack exhibition at a formal party, was thrilling, and everyone applauded. And we always won with him at the helm of a sailboat, displaying intensity and focus, and giving concise orders.

Mom was quite adamant. Her assessment of my father was that he was an alcoholic and that she was the cornerstone of justice, truth, love, and liberty. Both my brother and I have told the following tale to numerous therapists. We were traveling from my grandmother's rice plantation in South Carolina back to New York City. The Blue Ridge Parkway was about to close because there had been a light snow. Father announced to my brother and me that he was going to test Mother's nerve. There we went, slipping and sliding, roaring dangerously down the road. Every therapist since asked what our mother did. Nothing, absolutely nothing.

I started drinking in high school; and in many respects, alcohol seemed to remove my fear, boost my confidence, and fix my stuttering. I stuttered when sober, but much less.

My graduating class at the prep school in NYC had read *The Real Thing* by Henry James, a literary exploration that confirmed my confusion. What you saw was not what you got. The exercise of discernment became critical.

The tragic aspect of the situation: I was a complete imposter. Attending an LSD lecture at the League of Spiritual Discovery in Greenwich Village and two days later, donning my Junior Cotillion evening clothes to party at the Plaza, I was a chameleon, transmitting colors that mimicked my environment.

The imposter issue for me was exacerbated by the tenuous basis for my parents' marriage. Mom, a St. Cecelia debutante from the Holy City of Charleston, fell in love with a New York financier. Dad, an Anglophile and socialite, was only a generation away from the Irish Jesuits and Tammany Hall. Yet to hear him talk about it, Irish Catholics were the bane of the earth. Mom wanted the big-city high life, and Dad wanted to be "to the manor born." The lie to the other person was not half as bad as the lie they lived. Their arguments became a family classic in the genre of Gillette fight of the week.

Mom, with agony brushed across her face, would exclaim that she endured genteel poverty during the Depression. *Sorry, Mom, if you have eight household servants and you go to a private school, you are not poor. Call it what you will; you are not poor. You might have a cash flow problem, but you are not poor.*

Father claimed to have been traumatized during the Depression by poor people spitting on him when the chauffeur drove him to school and when the Irish nurses forced him to change from being left-handed.

It was a delightful hotbed of mental and emotional dysfunction. If we didn't laugh, we would have gone insane, or so I thought. Well, at least we laughed. Example: My two aunts biting each other's breasts in an argument over the potato famine in Ireland and grazing on the front lawn in East Hampton to prove the Irish could have eaten grass instead of starving. Or when Uncle Leonard left his Park Avenue apartment wearing only a toga and carrying a cross on Good Friday. This was my nurturing ground, exciting and highly neurotic.

There I was, a confused, reticent adolescent who stuttered. But after a few drinks, no stuttering; and free and easy communication flowed with the opposite sex. Winner, winner, chicken dinner. Interaction with the fairer sex was simpler, making me feel normal and functional. The big surprise was that my cure would become my contagion.

In the late spring of 1967, I graduated from Trinity School looking forward to the anonymity of a large, state university.

My experience with school up to that point was without girls in the classroom and no women teachers. Mom was the only woman at home. There were thirty-six boys in my high school graduating class, most of us having been together all twelve years, etching them forever in my memory. A coed state university, however, had a lot of appeal. Getting lost in a big university with women was akin to Br'er Rabbit being thrown in the briar patch.

I fell in love with a young woman, Kristina, the stepdaughter of one of my father's friends. It was my first relationship. I was smitten. The love, care, and attention we shared were new to me. It was wonderful to be alive and to have purpose. We studied, experimented with psychedelics, had sex, went to Woodstock, attended anti-war rallies, and had more sex. Both from dysfunctional families, we focused on each other.

The relationship with Kristina was filled with passion until she uttered that most terrifying expression, "I need a little space." My world collapsed.

Even after three nights of no sleep, to knock me out, it took a combined shot of Thorazine and Valium from a shrink friend. Climbing out of it, I needed a friend and mustered the courage to knock on Kathryn's door.

I had seen Kathryn at many of the supper club functions and at campus protests. But one day, walking the path that circled her apartment building on Senate Street, she wore a red peasant blouse and bell-bottom hip-huggers. It was her perfect profile. Her jaw line possessed a symmetry, beauty, and arch that suggested Teutonic angel rather than Carolina coed.

Her blushed pink cheekbones contrasted with her magnificent blond hair, generating some sort of elemental chemical recognition of goodness. She was special. And that is why I knocked on her door.

It was too painful to spend time by myself. From the break-up with Kristina to moving in with Kathryn, I spent only three nights alone. If writing copy for Casanova, that would be one thing; but for balanced emotional health, it was a terrible idea.

My newfound relationship with Kathryn blossomed, and we shared two glorious years merging our minds, hearts, and bodies. Maturity showed me that our time together as young lovers was my fair share of life's bliss, and the remainder of my life was to trudge. Kathryn had been my soul mate, the woman who made me complete. But I lost her.

# Flashback

THE BEGINNING POINT FOR ME WAS THAT CALL to her thirty-one years ago after going into alcohol rehab. To get sober, I had to make amends. It had taken me over eight months to track her down by phone, fifteen years at that point since we had had any contact. Horrendously immature, selfish, and narcissistic. King baby: a maniacal egotist with a severe inferiority complex.

A deep sense of gratitude came over me that Kathryn had not had to experience my full descent into alcoholism with all the associated collateral damage. Hurting her with my abhorrent behaviors had scarred me. Kathryn was my second failed relationship. I was not worthy enough to be loved. Well, if you were looking for an inauguration into alcoholism, here was an excellent start. She had made the right decision to leave me.

Our relationship would never have made it. Today would not exist if we had tried to stay together.

My desperation level was mounting when Kathryn and I were in our college apartment. Her music was critical for her. She had an immense amount of talent. It allowed her to harness and focus her energy in a productive direction. And she did—without me.

I was a course away from graduation with no idea how to support myself or how to care for the woman I loved. For some, her leaving would be a wake-up call to change behaviors. Not for me. Time to draw and quarter myself daily while anesthetizing my pain.

When we had gone our separate ways, my drinking was just beginning to get established, and it really took off. I determined that my heart would never be broken again and, experimenting as a bachelor, endeavored to keep a rotating stable of lace, belt-notching my affairs like a gunslinger with kills. Vigilant cocksman: deceitful, shallow, and scared.

# West Africa

MY STINT IN THE PEACE CORPS IN WEST AFRICA nearly ended most of the sexual antics. A lot of my friends had to get medivacked out of Africa after screwing local women. Even though it was dangerous, when the American holiday drinking festivals commenced, abandoning all judgment, we male agricultural volunteers had contests on who could get banged for the least pay. Once with only two sugar cubes, I won.

To pass the time, I had developed a "meaningful relationship" with a chimpanzee at a bar in Sierra Leone. For one beer, it would sit behind me and pick through my hair for two hours. What a treat. No STDs and only the cost of one beer.

West Africa killed the last shred of my political idealism. Also, it killed my wanderlust. Humans had died by my hand or from my actions in a culture I couldn't understand, initiating a voyage into my own "heart of darkness."

There had been a theft in the village where we were building a warehouse for rice storage. The chief had promised there would be no stealing. My complaint that concrete was missing caused the chief to hire a type of witch doctor called a "looking ground," who would identify the guilty parties. That done, the three people confessed. The chief advised me of our options: involve the national police, which would effectively be a death sentence, or the chief himself could dispense tribal justice. I opted for tribal justice, assuming there would a whipping like for the chief's wives when they were lazy during the rice harvest.

On the determined day, the thieves had been bound and staked out on the ground. Other Peace Corps volunteers arrived in the village to witness the machinations of local justice. The eldest son of the chief had mixed up four or five bags of concrete. Slowly and with apparent delight, the chief's son spread the concrete over the three criminals. By the end of the day, two had died, and the third had burns all over his body. The villagers enjoyed the day's entertainment. I left and got insanely drunk.

# Seattle

AFTER THE PEACE CORPS AND UPON MY BROTHer's suggestion, I settled in Seattle, Washington, my initiation to "adult" life, offering a geographical buffer to the proximity of our parents on the East Coast. Started selling real estate, a magnificent slot for me to fester and grow, a young, dynamic drinker with the mark of Cain. I dated another broker, Marsha, a New Englander, who was incredibly bright, and we clicked. Way too immature, we got married anyway. Got promoted and managed an office of forty sales associates. One month before she was to deliver our son, I quit my job. Luckily, Merrill Lynch Relocation called. This would develop my vocation for the next twenty years.

The baby was born, requiring me to put away my own childish behaviors. There was one problem: how to be an adult? Lacking substance and strategy, I was an empty suit.

Our marriage was pleasant for a while with a number of dynamic friends, cocktail parties, and weekend getaways. It was sort of an upper middle-class version of Toys for Tots. I co-owned with my brother a forty-foot, double-ended, cutter sailboat. The only disturbing issue was the correlation of sailboat racing and being horribly drunk.

I loved fatherhood with son Sam even though the partying dissipated in direct proportion to expenditures on children. Annual daycare was more expensive than tuition at Harvard. The boat was sold, the theater subscriptions ceased, the cocktail parties became infrequent, and concert attendance went by the wayside. I remember my father shouting out one of Zorba the Greek's answers to the question, *Are you married?* "Yes, wife, children, house: the full catastrophe."

We named our second child Matthew after St. Matthews, South Carolina, where we had been visiting friends living in an eighteenth-century coach house on the Old Charleston Highway. Our bedroom did not have air conditioning, and it was hotter than hell, too hot to sleep. What were we going to do? On the way back to Seattle, my wife announced that she was giving up smoking and drinking, and that she was pregnant. Nine months later, Matthew was C-sectioned into this world.

The boys were easy. It surprised me how much could be learned from their unpretentious behaviors. A pediatric nurse we employed for weekends away from home complimented us for having all the benefits of children without any of the usual problems.

Business kept me on the road and away from home 50 percent of the time. I trudged my way through scads of shitty real estate markets throughout the Pacific Northwest. As brokers wined and dined me, my consumption of alcohol increased. Weekends were dedicated to home. I rejected numerous proffered love affairs, puffing myself up as the paradigm of contemporary male virtue. My Protestant ethic was also ringing alarms in my head as bribes came my way, a witness to brokers making book on sporting games, squeezing vendors for kickbacks, and defrauding the VA and FHA. For a brief while, there was the illusion of purity. What a farce.

I jumped at a promotion to manage the disposition of all real estate assets in the Midwest at the company's regional operation in St. Louis, Missouri. Although this region was the slowest real estate market in the United States, our office continually achieved the best results. Under my management, our performance rocketed. The ivory tower of corporate was impressed.

# St. Louis, a Confluence of Rivers

A 1904 TUDOR HOUSE IN NEARBY CLAYTON, A suburb of St. Louis, fit the bill for the family, but something was wrong. Was it my relocation from the West Coast and the absence of an ocean? We had found for the kids a private school in Clayton. My job at Prudential was going swimmingly, and we joined the neighborhood and community.

It had cost a fair amount of money to have the hardwood floors refinished in our Tudor. Our youngest son, walking up the stairs with a bowl of cereal, spilled it all over the shiny wood. My automatic reaction was to scream—but not for long. Lightning bolt. I was behaving exactly like my father, which I'd sworn I would never do. Alcohol was suspect. The void in my chest was exponential.

The Episcopal Church we had joined in St. Louis had arranged "newcomer foyers," a.k.a., dinners at homes hosted by congregants, where controversial topics were assigned for discussion. The dinner at our house was to be "drugs and alcohol," a topic that dismayed me, hinting it would necessitate extra bottles of scotch. There could be a run on my personal stash.

Rather, nobody drank a drop. No liquor, no sherry, no wine, no nothing. What a shock. This was very different from the "Whiscopalians" of the eastern seaboard. Our church had scheduled Peter F., a congregant who was also a topic specialist. He explained the nature of addiction and the functions of a local treatment center. The primary focus: alcohol.

I played devil's advocate to the abstinence argument by citing "genius" friends of my dad who had been in Princeton's Advanced Study group. One climbed off the ambulance gurney and said, "If you think you are taking me to the hospital to die without a toddy, you have lost your fucking mind." He fixed a drink, climbed back on the gurney, went to the hospital, and died.

Peter F. was very gracious. After the gathering, he approached me about my conspicuous attitude concerning alcohol, adding that if he could ever be of assistance, to please call him day or night. I tucked his card in my wallet, deliberately segregating it from the usual business detritus. Several weeks passed before retrieving his card from my billfold. Everything was unraveling. After an argument with my boss during a company retreat, she suggested considering the possibility that I had a drinking problem.

Upon my return, I called Peter F., who arranged for an assessment meeting during the next day's lunch hour. They gave me a test. Only twelve questions. I got nine. If you get more than three, you might have a problem. More than five, full-blown alcoholic. Gee…nine. Hmm. The counselor asked about experimentation with other drugs; and after my twenty-minute monologue, his eyes looked like the surprised Buckwheat of the *Little Rascals*. He picked up the phone and asked, "Do we have a bed?"

Thirty days later, rehab released me, a novitiate in sobriety like a Boy Scout with a bit of training, thrown into the wild to survive. As a harbinger of life in sobriety, my wife informed me that as we moved forward, she would be drinking for two. I had little idea that recovery would chart the direction of my life.

My own alcoholism and my father's had polluted my life, making me rethink most of my history, trudging along with only the slightest inkling how long that journey might be. Many professionals, therapists, shamans, priests, and healers would be brought into the arena of self-examination. There were issues: family of origin, self-esteem, maniacal ego, an absolute host of shit, on top of getting my career back on track while being a husband and father. My "Boy Scout" rehab gave me a blueprint, but more than anything, it gave me a sense of hope and even optimism.

The first physical manifestation of hope post-rehab was a man named Jim M., sober five years. He became my mentor and guided me through the cliffs and mountains, the way the goddess Athena helped Telemachus discover his father's fate.

Unlike Odysseus, my father was not lost in the Aegean; he was navigating denial.

Dad's alcoholism was unlimited, and it seemed that he was always "under the influence." During Dad's third rehab in West Palm Beach, his counselor told me that in his thirty years of experience, he had never witnessed denial this deep. In fairness to Pops, he did learn something. Some fellow alcoholics in his group therapy were commercial airline pilots. Dad left treatment and took the train back to Southampton, saying, "Flying is too dangerous. Not only are the pilots loaded, but they're also taking drugs." Incredibly charismatic and bright, Dad dealt with the sociocultural obligations by drinking. Alcoholism skippered his destiny.

Jim M. taught me how to love myself and, in doing so, to come to understand my father due to the nature of the disease within myself. Loving an imperfect being, one who did his best with what he had, I identified with his experience, learning to embrace his every character flaw. It took longer to learn to accept what love he was able to give at the time and to treasure all of it.

# *Atlanta*

A FEW MONTHS INTO MY SOBRIETY, PRUDENTIAL purchased Merrill Lynch Relocation and shut down our St. Louis office. I was the only person offered a job with Prudential in Atlanta, and they kept advancing me. Business was on track as well as my performance leading a number of company initiatives.

We found a home in Dunwoody, which allegedly had the best schools in the metro Atlanta area. The subdivision had a swim and tennis club, offering kids plenty of physical recreation. Both of my boys were smart, and a lot of time was spent on their homework.

Providing time and toys for my boys was my new obsession. If a son expressed an interest in music, a guitar would appear. Biology brought Leica microscopes. Model trains precipitated the basement being finished for a railroad depot.

My childhood was completely different growing up in New York City, where any weekday outdoor interaction with my father consisted of walking to the liquor store. Consequently, when the store introduced free delivery, it upset me. Anything that interested me was fodder for my father's ridicule. First grade, I wanted to be a dancer. Father: "Oh, Christ, a fag." Third grade, I wanted to learn to play the violin. Father: "Oh, Christ, a fag." Sixth grade, I needed a glove to play baseball. Father: "You're too uncoordinated, and a glove won't help."

While my relationship with my kids was solid, my challenge was my marriage. Marsha was imbibing a lot more than she had in the past, creating problems for me in recovery.

When I had first moved to Atlanta, one of my male co-workers said, "There is an extreme oversupply of pussy based on demographics in Atlanta. Be prepared to take full advantage of it." His suggestion provoked me to crow that my marriage was happy. "That will change," he said. Five years later, his statement rang true.

I met a married woman early in her recovery, and we instigated a liaison. We were each other's ears for our problems at home. The situation required discretion, heightening the excitement. My ability to rationalize it reached its zenith. We mutually terminated the affair.

The boys were in private school and developing beautifully. Marsha and I both had jobs, providing ample economic security, but our marriage was tenuous. Everything looked like a Norman Rockwell painting, yet inside, I was dying.

My revolt from corporate life was slow. Although capitalism had nourished my ego and provided the economic foundation of my life for years, it disgusted me. Large corporations are akin to greenhouses: they could grow a lot, but it took a lot of "fertilizer."

Sitting in my basement next to the model trains, holding a 44 magnum, ready to end it all, I had an awakening: Quit the fucking job. Throw fate to the wind. My skill set could be more productive put to better use. Consult Marsha, and come up a plan.

# *Beaufort*

I WAS TEN YEARS SOBER, WORKING THE TWELVE steps and sponsoring a bunch of guys. Psychiatrists and psychologists all told me that my life questions were appropriate but that the answers were up to me. The serenity of the South Carolina Lowcountry called me back. My formative years on Wadmalaw Island had left an imprint as if genetic: my grandmother's unconditional love; the farm-fresh vegetables; shrimp right off the boat; and Helen, my beautiful nanny. After researching the public schools and having come up with a big zero, the challenge as a husband and father was to make sure the children would get a proper education. Private schools in Charleston and Beaufort were the best options. Charleston was too urban, and it would be too much like coat-tailing on Mother's social web. The Atlanta house sold, and we moved into a rental in Beaufort, enrolling the boys in a small private school with first-rate academic credentials.

Prudential hired me to do some consulting shortly after arriving in Beaufort. At $1,500 a day with a guarantee of six days a month, it was a very logical yes. This sure beat unemployment, and it would give me time to figure things out.

We bought a waterfront lot on nearby St. Helena Island, and construction of a house was soon underway. About two thirds of the way to completion, my past affair in Atlanta came to light. Marsha filed for divorce. What a lousy state in which to get divorced. Slow, very slow. It takes one year after submitting the initial paperwork. Settlement discussions would determine what was fair. She said for me to give her everything and go move in with my mother. We went to war.

At that juncture, having done some soul-searching, this verse spoke to me. It's from Julian of Norwich:

"Be a gardener.

Dig a ditch,

Toil and sweat

and turn the earth upside down

and seek the deepness

and water the plants in time.

Continue this labor

and make sweet floods to run

and noble and abundant fruits to spring

Take this food and drink

And carry it to God

As your true worship."

Neighbors had seen me caring for my yard, and they encouraged me to start a landscape company. After achieving master gardener status, I bought some equipment, hired a crew, and spawned Live Oak Landscaping (LOL).

Sons Sam and Matthew lived with me in the house that their mother and I had built, and barely six months after the divorce was finalized, Jane, the accountant at my boys' prep school, moved in. We had met in the rooms of recovery. She had been a high school beauty queen at the Rose Bowl parade—a classic California girl—yet she traveled on a British passport, and she enthralled me from the get-go.

On a trip that we took to see my father in Southampton, I proposed to her, and she accepted. Nine years into the marriage, she was getting pain pills from three different doctors, cooking the books on my landscape company for her personal benefit, and forging a number of documents required for term life insurance on me in which she was the beneficiary. In addition, the marriage had been long enough to entitle her to half of my assets. It turned out that she was extremely adept at smoke-and-mirror balance sheets and not as adept at ethics and substance recovery.

Later on, hearing she had died, I called my recovery mentor. How could I have loved her at one time but completely lack feelings surrounding her death? My recommendation is this: If you select a spouse from the rooms of recovery, you are selecting from the broken-toy box. While there are broken toys in all box sets, recovery box sets have a higher incidence of defects.

That was the end of the Beaufort chapter. I moved up to Charleston to live with my brother and to help with Mom. We had inherited some money after our dad died, allowing me a couple of years to spend playing on a motorcycle and hanging out with my boys as they wended their way through life. Two more relationships that came and went with me writing a check for them to go away.

# California, Key West, and Swinewood

WHEN THE INHERITANCE MONEY RAN OUT, MY cousin called me to move to Marin County, California. The daughter of my favorite aunt, she needed a nanny, chauffer, and cook for her eight-year-old twins, a girl and a boy, and I needed a job. My cousin's house was in a posh area, just down the road from George Lucas's Skywalker Ranch. My bedroom opened to a beautiful pool surrounded by citrus and eucalyptus trees.

The twins had a lot of extracurricular activities, like choral groups, gymnastics, and water polo. My cousin had divorced their father prior to conception, which was done in vitro. What? Don't ask; I couldn't possibly explain. She had another beautiful and bright daughter who was away at college during my nanny years.

My original reason for going there to help my cousin was to have a job, but our friendship got out of balance. She had no real spiritual yearnings, seeming more committed to materialistic endeavors. Keeping my focus on the kids helped to avoid ego conflicts. This lasted four and a half years.

During my time in California, my mother died. What a comfort to me to have been able to visit her several times back and forth, and even to see her right before she died. I renovated and rented out the house she left me in Mount Pleasant, South Carolina.

This meant that upon leaving California, I didn't have a place to live. My brother offered to share his "abode" with me—which was a dashing, Hinckley Bermuda forty-yawl sailboat named *Wunjo*, moored in Mount Pleasant. Living on the boat was enjoyable until we got underway. At sea, my older brother, Stephen, an ex-Special Forces officer, morphed into Captain Hook.

We started out in November and sailed down to Key West for the weather. The sunsets were beautiful; the winter climate was mild. The cruise ships were filled with thousands of dreadful tourists waddling down Duval Street taking selfies and spending money while predatory Lebanese gold merchants and Afghani t-shirt salesmen barked. Early every morning, the fire department hosed down the main drag to wash away the puke from the previous evening. A fitting microcosm of the Key West scene was the Anchors Aweigh Recovery Club, diagonal to The Lost Weekend Liquor Store.

After a month and a half in Key West, Stephen got tired of me. It was inevitable that my sojourn on his vessel would be limited. A backup plan was already in place in rural South Carolina: my friend Bryan's pig farm.

Swinewood Farm welcomed me in late February, where my landscaping skills were put to work caring for the yard, installing a vegetable garden, and exposing me briefly to animal husbandry. Though, to be frank, the pigs were pigs, and I impatiently watched the clock awaiting my Mount Pleasant tenant's short-term lease to expire.

The Swinewood philosophy of pigs—there were two varieties. There were Ossabaw pigs, which Spanish explorers left on the Georgia Sea Islands, and there were Nigerian potbelly pigs. Once the Nigerian potbellies were introduced to the pens, the Spanish Ossabaws implemented and enforced apartheid. One day, a Nigerian sow died giving birth to five piglets. A dominant Ossabaw sow lay down to nurse those piglets. I thought this was the beauty of nature, the continuity of life. Wrong. She was fattening them up. Three days later, the Ossabaw sow ate the entire orphaned litter of Nigerian piglets for lunch. Maybe the radicals of the sixties were right: cops were pigs. Maybe the feminists of the seventies were right: men were pigs. Maybe pigs eat their young naturally. Or maybe the sow realized her body would not support nursing, and she decided to make lemonade out of lemons. The state of apartheid ended with the inevitable inbreeding, and each new pig had the best of both categories.

# Mount Pleasant

AT LONG LAST, SEPTEMBER BROUGHT ME TO MY now-tenant-free home on the tidal estuary in Mount Pleasant, South Carolina. Preferring named estates to numerical addresses, I named my new digs Shady Grove. African rice planter, drunk executive, sober executive, gardener, nanny, sailor, pig farmer, gardener again, and now, nothing. Solitude. What a relief.

With only a bed, a few chairs, and a dining room table in the cottage, it was going to be a Spartan existence. A bicycle was my only transportation, and I had staked out a local recovery group reachable on two wheels.

The grocery store was a half a mile away; my doctor, three miles; and a hospital, less than a mile. If you must carry your groceries home in a backpack on a bike, never buy a watermelon or potato chips.

If there were honesty in a job interview, it would have gone like this: *John, why do you want a job for the Wallaby Convenience Corp?* "I don't, but I need the money. It's really impressive that you sell alcohol, tobacco, salt foods, sugar goods, caffeine, gambling, and gas all under one roof. It's what America and the new world order need. You really put to shame the addiction cartels of Central and South America the way you have been able to finance your distribution networks." Minimum wage it was.

My family had given me some spare furniture, an additional bed and chest of drawers to complete the guest room. I had no way of knowing at the time that a year later, love would be my first guest.

# The Weekend

NOT TO REHASH THE WEEKEND, BUT AS KATHRYN was about to walk out the door, she pivoted, strolled to the deck, and said, "This is a such a beautiful view; what an ideal place to write." I told her that one of my earlier tenants had never lived in the house. He simply kept a desk and a laptop here, and he only came over to work on his novel.

Kathryn remarked, "Let's write *our* book."

"Now, that's an idea. I need something to do," I replied.

No sooner than Kathryn had left the house, my recovery mentor was listening me elucidate the past forty-eight hours. "That sounds just like the movie I've been watching," he said.

"What movie is that?" I asked.

"*Casablanca.*"

My brain roared to life like a Ferrari's engine preparing to race. There were differences for sure. No sulking-little-boy behavior like Bogie, and my time frame was much longer than his had been. I drank for fifteen years trying to alleviate the pain of losing Kathryn. Rick and Ilsa (Bogie and Bergman) were only separated a year and a half from when he left Paris to her arrival in Casablanca.

# *Home Again*

THE MORNING AFTER KATHRYN'S DEPARTURE,
her email awakened me with her poem, "Eternal Estuaries":

"I left my toothbrush by the sink near the sweet bay
magnolia bloom and bamboo branches you arranged
After forty-seven years, we rewrote that chapter of our lives
I cry myself to dream now
Days and nights are one and the same
My mind keeps squeezing for space
Pushing hard against itself
For more and more joy
Even though my chipped toenail polish
Stares back at me,
Vacation is not over."
Our emails resumed but with a heightened vigor.

*On August 21, 2016, at 2:05 p.m., JohnDowdney1@getmail. com wrote:*

I was reading a physics article that described theoretical wormholes that tunnel through space and time and connect black holes, distant galaxies, and entangled particles. I went through one with you these last few days and discovered again the complete beauty and bliss of unconditional love. Be safe, and continue with the music of yourself. Hugs and love, John

*On August 21, 2016, at 11:19 p.m., KathrynScheldt1@getmail.com wrote:*

My dear John, it sounds fascinating and for sure is a mystery. Most everything that exists is way beyond my comprehension. I think love definitely fits in as the supreme mystery.

What you said about re-discovering unconditional love really grabbed me…closing that door while holding on to the thread. It ain't easy. I've always been a risk-taker by nature. I simply want every possible bit of this life. I don't think I will ever outgrow a desire for more. And then, there's the music of the spheres, which I am sure fits in with wormholes connecting the fibers of our being and pulling us here and there. Damn it all…this isn't making sense anymore, if it ever did.

John, I know you, and I have done a lot of soul-searching over the years and will continue to attempt to understand more and more what it all means, having those glimpses. Our time together was a touchstone with those shared years of youth, and seeing you as you are now is impossible to put into words. You know I wish you all the love and happiness you deserve.

As the vacation comes to a close, I thank you again for the wonderful visit and your fantastic hospitality. I'll give a holler from the road tomorrow when I get south of Atlanta.

Below is a quote my therapist gave me years ago. You may know it, but it is one of my faves and seems relevant. Keep holding on to the thread. Love, Kathryn

"The Way It Is"
There's a thread you follow. It goes among
things that change. But it doesn't change.
People wonder about what you are pursuing.
You have to explain about the thread.
But it is hard for others to see.
While you hold it you can't get lost.
Tragedies happen; people get hurt
or die; and you suffer and get old.
Nothing you do can stop time's unfolding.
You don't ever let go of the thread.
—William Stafford

The synchronicity of the *Casablanca* idea supercharged us. Within two days, we had both watched the movie again and downloaded the scripts. We were burning up our cell phones, which needed recharging by noon. We played with a variety of ideas as we drew parallels between the movie and our story. We planned to develop an outline or storyboard to maximize our effort and productivity, which required time together.

Even though her husband would be in Italy, he said he was cool with the idea. I would plant a series of camellias to pay for the journey.

# *Fairhope*

MY OCTOBER DRIVE TO FAIRHOPE, ALABAMA, BE-
came incredibly boring after the right turn at Jacksonville,
Florida, heading toward the Panhandle. Scrub oaks and
pines for four hundred miles made me weary. Roaring across
the interstate, reviewing the purpose of the journey in the
background: complete the storyboard, plant the camellias,
and continue to show gratitude. We had bared our souls
to each other only a month before, and getting hurt was a
possibility. I was going to reconnoiter. High propriety was
to be observed.

Kathryn's home was like herself: eclectic and life affirming.
Lots of art everywhere and photographs of her, a cross between
a perfect model from the Eileen Ford Agency and a prima don-
na from Cirque du Soleil. The home was bathed in a feminine,

sophisticated sensuality. Sight, smell, and texture all tangoed together to heighten awareness.

Kathryn and I focused on the book. Initially, we threw our ideas on colorful Post-its, taping them to the Mandarin-red dining room wall in a patchwork: peaches in Macedonia, young love on Patmos, peeing out the window in Zagreb. After two hours, we had run out of wall space. We embraced each other through our expressed thoughts, astounded at the uniformity of our memories.

A primal dance of thoughts, feelings, and desires slowly combusted. The physics were in place for the genesis of fire. You could almost smell smoke. The tremendous physical attraction was definitely there, but this was a broader sense of the word love—no longer merely about me. Kathryn was of utmost significance. Am I too old? Could I possibly get it right? Could I recommit to this woman at this stage in my life? All I could possibly offer her is love.

It was apparent that my resources could not support her in the manner to which she had become accustomed. Not only lifestyle, it was healthcare, international mobility, quality of food, etc. It would benefit her to stay right where she was. She had an assortment of friends and a large, extended family. She was financially comfortable, and she had plenty of freedom.

I revealed my inner thought processes to Kathryn. We discussed having an affair, and the issues of truth and deception were tossed about. My first marriage had imploded after breaching that line of truth by deceiving. We needed more time to think about it.

Reserve ruled the day, although our dialogue became more playfully risqué. In one exchange, I said, "Kathryn, if I had my druthers, I'd fuck you till you're blind."

She smiled and quipped, "I've always wanted a seeing-eye dog."

This made me throw my head back, bellowing in Falstaffian laughter. Not today, not here, not now; but that thought could never be erased.

After this, we exchanged a lot of camellia flower photos, vibrant colors, pink perfection, rose dawn, peppermint candy, and other stripper names sent daily through the cell phones. The wildflowers of our respective geographies communicated. This was much safer than in my earlier relationship as a student with her when I dressed like a ninja, went to public rose gardens to steal flowers at night, carefully removing all the thorns to prove the purity of my love. Ah, the romantic idealism of a young thief.

The next month in November, Kathryn and all her siblings made a pilgrimage to her father's home in Pennsylvania for his ninetieth birthday. On her way back to Alabama, she swung through South Carolina for a second visit here. We had spent the last two months talking daily and writing our story, and we would work on it again together.

We had numerous discussions about what might be evolving in the future. In my early corporate days, the headquarters referred to me as a gunslinger, making decisions with a minimum of information. My offer was to love her and take care of her to the best of my ability and to split my Social Security with her, cautioning her to think about what was sitting in front of her. My dream was to age with her until eternity.

Of course, this is offset by lottery logic: You can't win if you don't play. Most of us can't or won't change our attitudes or emotions in search of that soul mate. We can become too tired or emotionally infirm to continue the quest. We can be terrified of another rejection. Rejection for me is like salt on a slug: complete annihilation.

By the following April, her divorce was final, and she moved to Shady Grove. After a warm, enveloping hug, you have never seen two mature adults shed their clothes so quickly. As we held each other in erotic bliss, staring into each other's eyes, she transformed into that twenty-year-old nymphette. Not a line or a wrinkle.

# Life in Shady Grove

SHE'S BEEN HERE FOR OVER A YEAR. THE EARLY morning light brightens the springtime marsh. The marsh bunny's ears are electric orange in stark contrast to the peacefulness that pervades Shady Grove. The only discernible movements are the kairotic undulations of the tide change at water's edge: full, ebb, and everything in between. Kathryn is asleep, her face a mask of beauty reflecting the colors of dawn like a fine piece of Carrara marble.

Daylight continues to brighten, and the tide rises. Every morning when I wake up and see her first thing, I'm an exuberant eight-year-old on Christmas morning all over again, and every day is live musical theater.

There are thousands of stories about former lovers reconnecting, few in which the clock has passed half a century. We are two human paradoxes that have come together twice, and between the conjunctions are decades of struggle. Learning about our "character defects" and "shortcomings," we took separate paths and each made it to the mountaintop.

A breeze sways through the marsh grass. I fetch another cup of coffee. The caffeine kicks my brain into high gear, searching deep archives for uncorrupted data. In the alcoholic era, data corruption was a real issue.

If you follow any path from basically any starting place, you would wind up exactly where you need to be, provided you utilize a few simple ideas. Love yourself. Understand the corpus of social and cultural programming composing the software of your operating system. Experiment and learn. Make mistakes, fuck up, and relish being human. Love the beauty of imperfection. Simple but not easy. I've spent close to a lifetime practicing and practicing.

A red fox silently crouches his way through my backyard, and it's thrilling that wild animals continue to inhabit the neighborhood. Shady Grove gives them shelter. A warm sense of peace descends.

Ever since the college days, Kathryn has possessed a body consciousness that seems to be a hybrid of mime, contemporary ballet, and pole dancer. The secrets of the Universe to be appreciated and discovered are represented in her being, physically and spiritually. The struggle for me is getting the "I" out of the way. Kindness to people is an expression of gratitude for what God-Nature gives us. Namaste.

The whole aging thing is a challenge: more effort for fewer results. It runs contrary to our experience in our younger years.

To offset this daily degeneration, Kathryn and I have implemented a regime of massages. Mine is in the morning. In the evening, she takes a long soak in the bath. After she is dry, she lies down on the bed to be rubbed with scented oil: back, legs, flip over, chest, abdomen, neck, and head. And, last, the feet. Half the time, she is asleep before the finale. Old folks need more rest.

This is a very simple way to say that I want you to feel your best, and I love who you are, every single, fucking cell, or as we say in our text messages, ESFC. ESFC has become the code of conduct. My job is to love whatever has come from this roll of god's genetic dice: Kathryn. Doesn't mean tempers don't flare. Doesn't mean opinions get stuffed. At this point, I want the whole enchilada.

Way back on Patmos, when Sinjin the cat fell into the well and Kathryn became hysterical, her codependence with animals was in plain sight. During my visit to Fairhope, her cats, both rescues, made themselves scarce. They scooted from covered safety to covered safety, seeming to me just a little bit neurotic. Kathryn had shared with me her analysis of their respective personalities: Jezebel, grand dame of the Ragdoll breed, seventeen years old, dowager hump with attendant arthritic hind legs; Sprocket, feral street urchin, dragged by a truck as a kitten, discrete deformities, ginger striped cat with a face sporting a smidge of aristocratic lineage.

When Kathryn arrived with her felines emerging from their carriers, Jezebel looked like a lesbian Long John Silver who had been at sea for five years, and Sprocket was a speed freak gone awry. Individual therapy plans would be required for each cat.

Sprocket had played his gender card with Kathryn, and she had let him get away with it. His insolence was insufferable. After all, I still had my balls, and he didn't. He got enrolled in my Gentleman's School for Cats, bypassing Latin declensions of nouns and focusing on manners. Courtesy was going to be his lube of life. Vocal training helped convert a snarling "Get the fuck up and open the door" meow into a cheerful "Let me express my catness in the wild, please, Father" meow.

Kathryn had a cat door installed, much to my dismay. Within thirty seconds after the completion of the installation, Sprocket bolted through his door and, in a mere minute, proudly re-entered with a sizable snake dangling from his mouth, ergo my concern.

In challenging circumstances like this, I couldn't possibly modify his behavior to make him uncat-like. That would be unnatural. A philosophical approach afforded the best solution. What would a gentleman do? The answer came almost immediately: catch and release. The training took a solid month. Philosophy and theory of catch and release were discussed, complete with showing Sprocket charts and graphs, delineating small steps that would result in the desired action. If Sprocket made that horrid, guttural cry, indicating that he had caught something, that required me to bound out of the house with a treat in my hand. I would put the treat down, and he would release his prey to get the treat. By month's end, he was a graduate.

Having had a couple of wives made me aware that women spend a lot of time in the acquisition of their various attire and putting it all together. However, I was not prepared for "Miss Cuteness." Back on Patmos, our entire wardrobe consisted of shorts, bell-bottom hip-huggers, t-shirts, and swimsuits that would all fit in one small suitcase. With my move to Shady Grove, I jettisoned my corporate suits and other clothes that no longer fit my current lifestyle. Kathryn, on the other hand, remained prepared for any event from dining at the castle with the queen, to performing a concert in Nashville, to lounging on a chaise in Portofino. On target, always.

Kathryn's siblings refer to her as the Original Miss Cute. It's not just the clothes; it's the whole package. Body, mind, heart, and spirit. Not to mention the eight wardrobe containers that she brought with her. Those were just the start. There were six boxes filled with potions, creams, oils, fragrances, loofahs, and brushes. Lipsticks...fifty shades of red. Once, I asked her why she rarely went without makeup except at home. Kathryn said, "I like to get dolled up just a little bit. It makes me feel good." My Miss Cute is grace, élan, and finesse.

# *Finale*

TWO YEARS IN A TOTAL STATE OF BLISS. TO OB-
serve this beautiful woman mature with the inevitable gentle wrinkles, accents from the sun on her skin, and platinum
streaks emerging through a bale of blond on her head is sub-
lime. Signposts for wisdom. There's a hotness to youth, but a
woman of a certain age, driven by love, is the epitome of the
gender. As a siren, she continues to sing and entrance me. I
have baptized her the mother of all nymphettes.

Even though the humid Southern winter hides a cold
punch, the cottage at Shady Grove stays cozy. The fireplace
embers radiate curative properties to our aging bodies while
the cats compete for the prime warming areas. Our camellias
provide color, offsetting the occasional Berlin-gray sky.

Like the double helix of DNA, our thoughts and lives
have twisted around each other into a beautiful spiral as we

travel through time. Kathryn and I are separate strands coming together physically and psychically, creating one thread to which we both stay connected. We see our spirals at the beach in the conch shells, in the perseverance of the wave as it arches into itself, and in the blooming garden at Shady Grove. We are the force of the molecular bonds that gives us adhesion and cohesion.

# ABOUT THE AUTHORS

KATHRYN AURELIA SCHELDT, author, is an international-
ly acclaimed songwriter and recording artist with seven CDs of
original songs. Her published books are: *The Guitar Songbook
for Music Therapy*, *Six Neapolitan Songs for the Classic Guitar*,
and *The Quilt and the Poetry of Alabama Music.*

A former music professor (Queens University of
Charlotte, University of South Alabama), Scheldt holds a
master's degree in music. Her performances include Bluebird
Cafe in Nashville, Ernest Tubb Midnight Jamboree, Southern
Festival of Books, Alabama Writers Forum, and Thacker

Mountain Radio. Her song "Last Shrimp Boat" anchored the soundtrack for *In the Path of the Storms*, an Emmy-winning documentary.

JOHN HEYWARD DOWDNEY, first-time author, springs from illustrious literary and historical giants. On his paternal side: *The Edwin Emerson Family Papers*; Abraham Dowdney, representative from New York; and Edward Fitzgerald, British author and translator of *The Rubyait* of Omar Khayyam. Dowdney is a descendant of Thomas Heyward, Jr., South Carolina's signer of the Declaration of Independence; and his maternal lineage also boasts DuBose Heyward, author of *Porgy* and *The Country Bunny*.

Dowdney attended Trinity School in Manhattan and graduated from the University of South Carolina with a bachelor's degree in English literature. He spent several years in the Peace Corps in West Africa followed by twenty-five years in corporate America. When he retreated from the corporate tower, he became a gardener on one of South Carolina's sea islands.